A Photo Journal: Seldom Seen Sights

ASIA
Edition

BY
KENNETH MICHAEL BROPHY

Copyright © 2008 by Kenneth Michael Brophy. 47156-BROP

Library of Congress Control Number   2008904688

ISBN: Softcover   978-1-4363-4519-4
        Hardcover   978-1-4363-4520-0

All rights reserved. No part of this book may be reproduced or transmitted in any form or by any means, electronic or mechanical, including photocopying, recording, or by any information storage and retrieval system, without permission in writing from the copyright owner.

This book was printed in the United States of America.

To order additional copies of this book, contact:
Xlibris Corporation
1-888-795-4274
www.Xlibris.com
Orders@Xlibris.com

Table of Contents

Dedication Page 5

i. **Author's Note & Introduction** 6

I. **Seldom Seen Sights of Malaysia**: Kuching in the Daylight, Kuching at Night, Sarawak beyond Kuching, National Parks of Borneo, Batang AI National Park National Parks of Peninsular Malaysia 9

II. **Seldom Seen Sights of the Philippines** 163

III. **Seldom Seen Sights of China** 179

IV. **Snapshot of the 2008 Beijing Summer Olympics** – a Peek at the Games of the XXIX Olympiad Venues, What to See and Do in Beijing and Other Interesting Sites. 235

Acknowledgements and Photo Credits 247

About the Author 248

To all the victims and those who suffered tragic losses
resulting from the 2008 cyclone and floods in Myanmar,
horrific earthquakes that shocked central China and
devastating Typhoon Fengshan that capsized a ferry
with 700 onboard off an island in central
Philippines with few survivors found.
And on a more pleasing note, to my first granddaughter,
the spark of the 21st century,
pumpkin number 3—Madelyn (Brophy) Mead.

Author's Note and Introduction

Welcome to the first-ever edition of *A Photo Journal*: *Seldom Seen Sights*. On behalf of the editors and publishers of Xlibris, my family, friends, and collaborators, we invite you to relax and enjoy this special Asia Edition. Everywhere on the planet, from tiny remote villages like *LiJiang Old Town* to crowded, pollution-choked industrial cities like *Beijing* or *Manila*, there are something curious to attract the observation of a traveler and seduce the lens of a camera. Camera seduction sometimes produces *seldom seen sights.* Take a stroll through this book and see for yourself. Asia is a vast place; thus, for economy of scale, we have chosen three countries to highlight in this Asia Edition of *Seldom Seen Sights*—Malaysia to help celebrate its fifty-year anniversary, China to applaud its first Olympic Games opportunity, and the Philippines because no one is sure how many islands they have—let's find out.

All of the text and the majority of the photographs in this—Asia Edition—are the creation of the author. Having traveled to 118 countries, in the past twenty-five years, while visiting over a thousand national parks and scenic wonders of the world, I built up a collection of what I believe are seldom seen sights. I'd like to share some of these with you. I am neither an expert photographer nor a great writer; it is reported, however, that my creations have pleased many. They sometimes capture the rare, the unusual, the unfortunate, the wonders of the world, simple but elegant rural lifestyles, and unique cultures. The people I chose to photograph are real, believable, and sometimes touching. They are not models, but simple people going about their everyday lives. To measure success, and please myself, the photos and text must capture some evidence of raw nature or the human drama, with a sympathy and compassion that leaves the viewer or reader feeling something and walking away a better person for having viewed the photos and read the text. Study the faces. Can you find innocence, pain, suffering, hardship, grief, joy, happiness, kindness, or love in any of them? If so, *A Photo Journal*: *Seldom Seen Sights*—Asia Edition is in some small way a success.

For the past twenty-four years, I have often visited Malaysia, for periods of three to six months, to explore remote areas and encourage Malaysia to develop its national park system, similar to that of America's NPS. Today, Malaysia's national park system is the finest in Asia, with twenty-one world-class national parks and four Ramsar sites. (Incidentally, Malaysia comes in two fine pieces—East Malaysia and West Malaysia; they are separated by 625 miles of the South China Sea.) I often traveled and stayed with friends. Together, we trekked through dense jungle, climbed to Malaysia's highest peak (the highest peak in all of Southeast Asia, Mount Kinabalu 4,100 meters (13,450 feet), sailed to remote islands with overnight stays on TV-made-famous *Survival Island*, slept on sandy beaches with leatherback turtles, hung on tight as express boats flew up the Rajang River through the rain forest of Borneo, and hiked the many national parks of Peninsular Malaysia (West Malaysia). We hope to share some of those experiences herein.

Many parts of Borneo Malaysia (East Malaysia) are remote, seldom explored, and home to somewhat primitive Dyak and Iban native tribespeople—the poison dart, blowpipe, head-hunter guys—as well as, the *man of the jungle*, the endangered orangutan. *A Photo Journal*: *Seldom Seen Sights*—Asia Edition shares some of the Dyak and Iban culture and current-day lifestyle with you and provides a glimpse or two of the orangutan life in the wild.

Rain forests, wetlands, beachfront, volcanoes, and crater lakes are some of the wonders that will delight you when you visit some of the, over a dozen, fine Filipino national parks and reserves. With 7,101 islands, the Philippines boasts of having thirty-four thousand kilometers (twenty thousand miles) of shoreline, and much of that is sandy beach. Many of the islands are uninhabited, which you are welcome to explore. I have captured a few examples on camera and posted them inside.

In the past few years, I traveled throughout China eight times, for two weeks or more, by train, riverboat, express ferry, car, bus, plane, or just plan hiked, with the intent to visit many remote locations, national parks, and scenic wonders. I found China's national park system to be well organized, interesting, and places dedicated to protect the natural environment for future generations to enjoy. China's National Park System is emerging rapidly and promises to soon be one of the world's premium showcases of rich natural heritage. Some of China's breathtaking new national parks visited and illustrated herein include the following: Jade Dragon Snow Mountain National Park, Stone Forest National Park, Tiger Leaping Gorge National Park, Li River Scenic National Monument, Shangri-La National Park, and many other national historic and natural wonders. With a flip of a page, the reader will experience the following: a cable car sojourn to the top of a lofty mountain peak and glacier; an exciting outdoor theater musical production, with a cast of a thousand well choreographed, that competes with the finest Broadway productions; a descent to the depths of a roaring river gorge that is second only to the Grand Canyon in magnificence; explore fish-rich lakes; examine close-up exotic Oriental architectures, customs, sculptures, and dresses; and float aboard a star cruise ship along a mysterious river lined with high-rise pinnacles, often illustrated in traditional Chinese paintings, and fished daily by cormorant fishermen.

Inside the covers of *A Photo Journal*: *Seldom Seen Sights*—Asia Edition, you will find a short chapter on the 2008 Beijing Summer Olympics venues. China has spent billions on creating stadiums of architectural wonder. We would be remiss if we didn't share some of these remarkable architectural accomplishments with you. The author visited Tibet in 2007 and herein shares a few Tibetan photos. Today, Tibet is closed to visitors. Hopefully, in the spirit of China's Olympic committee commitment made two years ago to improve its human rights record, China will see fit to open Tibet's borders to tourist in time for the games.

For the armchair traveler, too busy to make the journey to these far-off places of wonder and beauty, or the many people in the world without the resources to do so, we hope *A Photo Journal*: Seldom Seen Sights—Asia Edition brings home to you some of the excitement, charm, adventure, and mystique of the Orient. Enjoy!

If you have taken the time to read this note, you have proven yourself to be someone who is interested in the beauty and wonder of our planet. As you flip through the remaining pages of this book, we challenge you to think of ways to help preserve and protect these beauties and wonders for future generations to enjoy. We leave you with some food for thought, ideas, hints, or suggestions we all can help implement to improve Malaysia's, the Philippines's, and China's environment, thus benefiting all of Asia and mankind. They are as follows:

1. outwit selfish-lobbied politicians
2. stop uncontrolled deforestation especially in watershed areas
3. prevent soil erosion
4. clean-up air and water pollution in major urban centers
5. prevent coral reef degradation
6. control increasing pollution of coastal mangrove swamps that are important fish breeding grounds
7. check desertification
8. breed and protect endangered species
9. eliminate hazardous wastes
10. obey the law of the sea
11. stop marine dumping
12. enforce ozone layer protection
13. internationally legislate against ship pollution and enforce the new laws foil the tropical timber tycoons that needlessly rape the rain forests encourage wetlands preservation and new growth
14. orchestrate a binding international nonwhaling, nondolphin fishing agreement

Seldom Seen Sights of
MALAYSIA

Kuching the Cat City

History

Malaysia broke off from the British Commonwealth and gained independence in 1957 by forming fourteen states. Initially, Singapore was one of the fourteen states. Made up of mostly Chinese citizens, Singapore didn't always agree with the Islamic views of Malaysia, so it formed its own country in 1963. The Malaysian flag is similar to the American flag and has fourteen red and white stripes; Malaysia still carries a stripe for Singapore. The largest of the thirteen states by land mass is Sarawak, which is located on the island of Borneo.

In the late 1830s, the sultan of Brunei owned all of Borneo when he came under attack by the native Iban tribes. The sultan heard of magnificent warships with powerful canons that were visiting what is now Singapore. The sultan visited Singapore and met Commodore James Brookes, British Navy. He convinced Brookes to come to Borneo and defeat the Ibans—the poison dart, blowpipe, head-hunter guys. Brookes easily defeated the Ibans. For his reward, the sultan gave Brookes what is today Sarawak. Brookes built a fortress named after his wife, Margarita; a governor's mansion; and British Courthouse in Kuching, Sarawak. All buildings are in good condition and can be visited today. He also set up a farming community about three hours' ride by express boat up the Rajang River, in what is today Sibu. He traded for several hundred Chinese indentured slaves to farm the land and grow rice, pineapples, etc.

Today, Sibu has a population of about two hundred thousand Foochow Chinese. Kuching, the capital of Sarawak, has a population of about one hundred thousand Hiananese, Hakka and Hokkien Chinese besides over one hundred thousand native Malays and Dayaks.

Geography

Malaysia is comprised of two main areas: Peninsular (West) Malaysia, which extends south from Thailand—at its tip is mainland Asia's farthest point south; and East Malaysia, which lies east of Peninsular Malaysia across 628 miles of South China Sea on the island of Borneo.

At 830 miles long (1328 kilometers) by 600 miles wide (960 kilometers), Borneo is the third largest island in the world, behind Greenland and Australia. Borneo is divided among three countries: Brunei, the smallest of the three; East Malaysia; and Indonesia's State of Kalimantan, the largest of the three which occupies 75 percent of Borneo's land mass. Sarawak and Sabah are the only two Malaysian states on Borneo.

Wildlife

Malaysia is known for the orangutan, eighteen species of hornbills, and over four thousand wild orchids, which grow in the rain forest, mostly in Borneo. Borneo and Indonesia's Sumatra Island are the last remaining stronghold of the orangutan, literally translated means *the man of the jungle.* The O-U (*Pongo pygmaeus*), however, is seldom seen in the wild, but can be seen at three wildlife reserves. One such excellent reserve is located thirty minutes drive from Kuching. Today, it houses twenty O-U orphans, from six months to twelve years that are being trained for reentry into the wild.

Travel to Malaysia

Most travelers from Western countries enter Malaysia via Kuala Lumpur International Airport. There are nonstop flights twice a week from New York's Newark Airport. KL, as the natives call the capital city of Malaysia, is a forty-five-minute express train ride from the airport. The train is a high speed, super high-tech express with KL its only stop. It is the best way to reach KL from the airport.
Kuala Lumpur International Airport is one of, if not the, finest airport(s) in the world. Once inside the international concourse, foreigners must take a one-stop train to the immigration,

baggage claim, and custom's main concourse. Push carts are available gratis (America needs to learn this handy practice) and can be taken to the express train platform. Usually there are no waits at the immigration passport counters—I waited for over an hour at London Heathrow Airport in June and July 2006, and nearly two hours in San Francisco, while its new concourse was under construction.

Kenneth's Picks—Seldom Seen Places to Visit in Peninsular Malaysia

1. **Kuala Lumpur** (A cosmopolitan modern city—capital of Malaysia with about three million people.)
    - Petronas Twin Towers— Once the World's tallest buildings (now the honor belongs to Burj Dubai) offer tours to its eighty-floor and modern basement shopping mall. Cuban, Syrian, Iranian, Lebanese—all sorts of international shops are present.
    - Orchid Garden—One of the world's finest orchid gardens with hundreds of species in bloom all year long.
    - Bird Park – A modern facility and an all-day affair with amphitheater live bird shows, thousands of birds, fishponds, waterfalls, food stalls, and fine restaurant serving spicy Malaysian cuisine.
    - Butterfly Park—the world's finest lepidoptera park.
    - Modern National Zoo and Aquarium
    - Petaling Street night market—The center of Kuala Lumpur's original Chinatown. Petaling Street maintains much of its traditional atmosphere, particularly at night when vendors spread their wares out on the street. While it is possible to purchase anything from gems and incense to toys and T-shirts here, enjoying the night market is really a matter of just wandering about and enjoying its sights, sounds, smells, and energy.
    - Historic British colonial buildings especially, my favorite, the old railroad station, still in use today. Its Moorish-style terminal was built in 1910; it is a charming, smart, elegant, classy building equipped with air-conditioned waiting halls, snack kiosks, money-changing booths, souvenir shops, restaurants, and a tourist information counter.
    - Try a sumptuous Malaysian buffet at night atop Asia's tallest space needle—the KL Tower.
    - All sorts of museums—My favorite is the National Museum and its beautiful lake gardens.

2. **Penang, Malaysia**—A beach resort, an hour's flight north of KL, with many five-star hotels, my favorite is the Shangri-La Hotel. Each hotel has several swimming pools, joined together by waterfalls or canals, lined with exotic tropical plants and flowers. Typical beach fun—parasailing, windsurfing, surfboarding, or bodysurfing. There are always lots of sunshine and beautiful sandy beaches. See Georgetown, a historic British fortress area and take in the Chinese temple of the ten thousand Buddhas—it really has ten thousand Buddha statues.

3. **Genting Highlands**—Take a one-hour bus trip from KL to about six thousand five hundred feet above sea level (two thousand meters) to Genting Highlands with its largest casino in Southeast Asia, eighteen-hole golf course, and theme amusement park. One day (eight hours) bus tour from KL runs about $60 US.

4. **Historic Malacca**—a seventeenth century historic Portuguese-Dutch trading community about an hours drive outside KL on the Straits of Malacca.

Kenneth's Picks—Seldom Seen Places to visit in East Malaysia, Borneo

1. **Kuching**—A Malay Islamic, Buddhist Chinese, and Hindu Indian community.
   - Riverfront walk – interesting views of life along the Sarawak River, still crossed today by six-person sampans. A modern boardwalk has been built on piers over the river that service fishing boats and a tour diner cruise ship. Along this mile stretch of riverfront are many souvenir and antique shops, food stalls, riverfront cafes, a Chinese history museum, exotic plant and flower gardens, contemporary sculpture, Brookes Tavern, a Chinese temple, the Holiday Inn and Hilton Hotel, and an amphitheater.
   - Fort Margarita—ride a sampan (fifty cents Malaysian) across the river and tour the fort and newly opened Orchid Gardens.
   - Visit the British Courthouse—now a museum.
   - Shop at the famous India Street with its exotic sights and smells of the Orient.
   - Visit the Sarawak Museum and Aquarium, one of the finest in all of Asia, in my opinion.
   - Cultural Village—a few minute outside Kuching is a micro snapshot of life in Borneo. All twenty-five ethnic tribes have a typical dwelling, staffed by tribe members in traditional dress, on display. Each day, a well-choreographed song, music, and dance performance is conducted at the village air-conditioned theater.

- Damai Beach Resort—Stay in a Tree House cabin with all modern luxuries.
- Bako National Park—(One of nineteen national parks in Malaysia) I have placed Bako National Park on my "top ten best parks in the world" list, which will appear in my new book: *The World's Greatest National Parks: How Well Do You Know Them?* From Kuching take a bus to a small fishing village and board a longboat (carved-out canoe with a small outboard motor and a tiny propeller mounted on a shaft that extends twelve feet from the stern of the canoe) for a spectacular thirty-minute journey to the island park. (Reservations are required, and all arrangements can be made from the Malaysian Tourist Bureau Office in Kuching). Bako NP is known for extraordinary variety and contrast between its immaculate secluded, sandy white coves and emerald green waters, and sea arches and sea stacks, to its high country dipterocarp forest, plants, and wildlife. Stay in your own quaint cabin along the beach, but beware of the very aggressive macaque monkeys. They are fierce. There is a camp store and canteen, which constantly gets robbed by the clever monkeys. Bring a hat, sunblock, and bug spray.
- Orangutan Reserve—About thirty miles outside Kuching, visit the reserve to see, touch, and smell these magnificent creatures.

2. **Express Boat Trip to Sibu**—Take an exciting aerodynamically designed, long and narrow express boat (a floating aircraft fuselage that skims along the water surface at forty miles per hour) sojourn to Sibu along the Rijang River. The three-hour journey follows the Sarawak River to its effluent, crosses the open water of the South China Sea to the Rijang River entrance, and follows it to Sibu. There is great shopping in Sibu as well as interesting pagoda-style Chinese buildings.

3. **Gunung Mulu National Park**—Mulu NP Resort is a splendid five-star hotel built on stilts over the jungle floor. It is constructed of teakwood and other Malaysian hardwoods found only in Borneo. Each night locals put on a cultural song and dance performance dressed in traditional native customs. Visit five caves, one with a river running through it, another with one million bats that come screaming out every evening at dusk, through a small opening, much to the delight of tourists. But, in my opinion, the best attraction at Mulu is the limestone pinnacles. To view the pinnacles takes three rugged days of excitement and adventure. First, take an exciting two-hour, upriver, high-speed longboat trip over rapids. During dry spells, be prepared to get out of the boat and shove it over the rocks and gravel riverbed. Next, take a four-hour hike, eight miles, through dense virgin rain forest; ford two rivers on the way, both have a wire rope pulled tightly across to hang on to and avoid being swept downriver. Lastly, spend an enjoyable night at Camp 5, located below the pinnacles in a beautiful lush valley four thousand feet above sea level (1,200 meters).

Sleep in an open-air hut (no walls, just a roof and a board raised two feet above the jungle floor to keep snakes away) and bath in a shallow cove on the bank of the Melinau River, the clearest water I've ever seen. Enjoy a wonderful Malaysian meal prepared by a gracious park ranger and his bride. It's up at dawn for another nice Malaysian meal before starting a rough, strenuous four-hour climb (3,300 feet vertical climb [one thousand meters]) to the top of Mount Gunung. It is a very steep path with dangerous canyon crossings made of wooden planks (six-inches wide [twenty centimeters]) and no handrails. There are a few vertical climbs where the park service has attached aluminum ladders to the rock surface. Once at the viewing platform, you discover a beautiful sight not found anywhere else in the world; hundreds of limestone pinnacles tower above the top of the forest canopy. The pinnacles stick through the treetops like the Golden Gate Bridge stanchions stick through San Francisco's fog. Well worth the journey.

4. **Mount Kinabalu NP, Sabah, Malaysia**—At 13,450 feet (4,100 meters) above sea level, Mt. Kinabalu is the highest mountain in Southeast Asia. It takes two days to reach the top with a well-trained guide. You spend the first night at 12,000 feet in bunkhouse-style accommodations. It's up at 2:00 a.m. to finish the journey to the top in the dark, so as to enjoy the sunrise over the South China Sea. It is a spectacular journey, which I highly recommend. Expect to see a variety of wild orchids and pitcher plants, which the locals call monkey cups.

5. **Batang Ai Longhouse Resort and National Park**—Hilton Hotel owns this resort and bills it as a "naturalist's paradise." It is built on an island, on a man-made lake, deep in the rain forest. From the Longhouse Resort, local tribe guides provide longboat day excursions to the national park, via a scenic river with a wonderful waterfall—they stop for a swim in Irup Waterfall pool—and a stop to visit an authentic longhouse. Guests may make arrangement to spend the night with the locals at the authentic longhouse. The area is home to over two hundred butterflies, many of which can be seen around the hotel swimming pool. Back at the resort, sample authentic Iban cuisine and Tuak—homemade rice wine. Then allow nature to serenade you to sleep with its noisy insect-critter lullaby. Save a few hours in the morning to hike with the hotel naturalist to the top of Batang Ai Island. The trail through the rain forest culminates with a walk above the treetops, on a man-made boardwalk suspended high above the jungle floor.

Malaysia's Magnificent National Park System

Above: A map of Malaysia's fine young national park system.

Situated in the heart of South East Asia, Malaysia sits on the equator and, as such, is blessed by plenty of sunshine and warm climate throughout the year with daily temperatures ranging around 30 degrees C (90 degrees F) in the lowlands to dropping to as low as 15 degrees C (60 degrees F) in the highlands. The constant warm weather and closeness to the sea are all it takes to create daily afternoon rain showers. As a corollary, Malaysia is covered by a magnificent rain forest that is endowed with many varieties of flora and fauna, natural resources and wonders. Malaysia's rain forests are indisputably the oldest primeval forests on the planet. They are dominated by upper canopy dipterocarp hardwood trees, some of which, such as the tualang, are the second tallest trees in the world at over one hundred meters (three hundred feet), and a lower canopy that is thick with lush vegetation including numerous varieties of bamboo and exotic fruit trees, e.g., breadfruit, rambutan, mangosteen, starfruit, and durian to name a few. Epiphytes such as ferns and rare species of orchids are abundant beneath the lower canopy.

Begun formally in 1969, Malaysia's national park system has grown to twenty-one world-class national parks and five Ramsar sites. Young as it is, nevertheless, it is perhaps the finest park system in Asia. The NPS has been created to protect the oldest primary rain forest, estimated at 130 million years old, its wildlife, wonders, and vast resources for future generations to experience and enjoy. Malaysia's national parks are treasure troves of rich natural heritage. The parks are home to the world's largest flower at one meter (three feet), the rafflesia, and the world's smallest squirrel, the pygmy squirrel. Both are difficult to view in the wild because the rafflesia stays in bloom for only one day, and the pygmy squirrel for obvious reasons. Several of the parks including Batang Ai NP, Mount Kinabalu NP, Bako NP, and Gunung Mulu NP have already been mentioned above. Some of the other more prominent national parks that are developed, in terms of services such as cabins, longboat river excursions, visitor centers, and ranger-guided tours are noted below (overall email for information or park accommodation reservations: pakp@wildlife.gov.my or phone 03-90752872):

- **Taman Negara**—Malaysia's first and largest in the country with 434,300 hectares of primary forest is located on Peninsular Malaysia. Comfortable cabin-style accommodations are provided by the NPS at the Park Headquarters in Kuala Tahan. Groups of long-tailed macaque and gibbon monkeys can be spotted in the lower canopy or on the ground inside your cabin going through your personal effects. Be careful, they can be vicious—carry a pocketful of pebbles. They'll scatter if you throw a few pebbles at them. The rare leaf monkey may also be spotted if you look carefully on the branches of the upper canopy. There are over 250 bird species inside the park including the indigenous rhinoceros hornbill. Barking deer, wild boars, tapir, tigers, and leopards have been spotted in the park.
- **Endau Rompin**—Located alongside two untamed rivers in Peninsular Malaysia, the Endau River and the Rompin River, the park is thick with cloud forest and home to the Bengal tiger and Asian elephant. For those interested in jungle trekking, there are many challenging hiking trails, cut through the dense jungle undergrowth by the elephants that are tunnel-shaped and led from the rivers to higher ground in the jungle. To satisfy those with a little "Indiana Jones" in them, these trails can be

dangerous due to the unpredictable nature of tigers, leopards, and elephants. Travel alone is not recommended. The park service offers excellent guided longboat river tours. The park offers the visitor a chance to meet some ancient tribespeople who have lived inside the park perimeter for centuries. They have subsistence privileges, which permit them to fish, gather, and hunt inside the park.

- **Tunku Abdul Rahman**—Comprises a group of islands located three to eight kilometers (two to five miles) off the coast of Borneo near Kota Kinabalu. The TV show *Survivor* was filmed on one of these offshore Borneo islands. *Webster* defines survivor as somebody who remains alive despite being exposed to life-threatening danger. You will not be in much danger on the exciting islands, but you will find plenty of adventures for the islands are rimmed by fascinating coral reefs, marine life including green sea turtles, dolphins, porpoises, and dipterocarp forests. The NPS has established twenty wood chalets, situated on a lush green slope overlooking the white-sand beach and turquoise-colored sea. All are set within a garden of tall swaying palms and exotic tropical plants in colorful bloom. E-mail: nature@kinabalu.net.my for reservations.

- **Turtle Islands**—The island's (pulaus in Malaysian) park lies forty km (twenty-four miles) north of Sandakan in the Sulu Sea off Sabah's east coast. It includes three islands: Selingan, Bakkungan Kecil, and Gulisan. Pulau Selingan is the world's main nesting island for the green turtles (*Chelonia mydas*), while the hawksbill turtles (*Eretmochelys imbricate*) enjoy the beaches of Pulau Guisan. Both species lay their eggs on the shore throughout the year. Turtle Islands National Park exists solely to protect these two species from extinction. Rangers live 24/7 on the islands to protect the eggs from poachers. It is a fine job the Malaysian government is doing through its National Park Service, Tourist Boards, and Departments of Conservation and Environmental Protection to protect endangered species. Accommodations are available on the islands for those who wish to stay overnight and witness the turtle nesting. Three units for twenty persons are available. Other camping arrangements can be made by emailing the following: cquest@tm.net.my.

- **Tanjung Datu**—Located eighty kilometers west from Kuching (forty-eight miles) on the Indonesian border with Sarawak, it is one of Malaysia's newest and smallest national parks. Situated in a mountainous region whose steep cliffs hug the shoreline, the park features swift-flowing rivers with crystal-clear pollution-free waters, beautiful white-sand beaches, and a shallow aquamarine rim reef with limited coral reefs. There are no accommodations inside the park; however, it is accessible by road within three and a half hours journey from Kuching.

The Wild Jungle Fruits of Malaysia

Over fifty varieties of wild fruits grow in the rain forests of Malaysia and are free for the taking. Malaysia's orangutans, hornbills, and local tribespeople all get their fair share. Wherever you travel in Malaysia, you are bound to come across stalls selling wild jungle fruits. Stop and buy some. They may look unusual, but they taste sweet and juicy.

Some of the most popular species are the following:

- **Durian**—Often called "king of fruits," it is the size of two large pineapples combined, as heavy as a bowling ball, could kill you if it fell on your head, is covered in sharp spikes and smells like the worst pair of sweaty sneakers. It smells so bad; in fact, most hotels in Malaysia ban guests from bringing durian into the hotel. Once you get past the tough, thorny cover, and that is no small feat, the fruit inside tastes like good vanilla custard.
- **Starfruit**—They have a greenish yellow color, appear translucent, and take on a starlike shape. They are tart.
- **Mangosteen**—The author's favorite. Mangosteens are endemic to Malaysia and Indonesia; they are the size of a tennis ball, have a maroon outer skin, and four to six berrylike clear white fruits inside. They are delicious. But be careful peeling the skin, the dark purple juice will stain your skin and clothes.
- **Rambutan**—Another endemic fruit of Malaysia and Indonesia, they are egg shaped with either a bright gold or purple reddish skin covered in long hair and are seasonal. The fruit inside is clear translucent, sweet, and succulent. Be careful, each piece of fruit has a tiny hard pit inside—the tooth-breaker variety.
- **Papaya**—Believed to be from South America, papaya is found throughout the Malaysian rain forest. It is a favorite of the local Malay tribes. Once you peel away the thin skin, you can almost eat it like an apple. Most people, however, cut the sweet, succulent fruit into many pieces that are usually eaten by hand.

KUCHING, MALAYSIA—Alias Cat City

1 & 2. In the late eighteenth and early nineteenth centuries, Chinese sailing ships—junkets—sailed up the Sarawak River to seek shelter from South China Sea storms or to trade. On the bow of the junkets was a single bay window that many thought resembled a cat's eye. The town was nicknamed Kuching, which in Chinese means *cat's eye*. Today, Kuching has many monuments to the cat.

3 & 4. Kuching's Riverfront is a great open-air meeting place with sidewalk cafes and exotic food stalls. There are no bridges across the muddy Sarawak River in the downtown area. Sampans take passengers across at about twenty cents a ride.

5. Not the friendliest-looking cats.

6. James Brooks Café & Pub on the Riverfront. In 1839, the sultan of Brunei owned all of Borneo when he came under attack by the native Iban tribes. The sultan heard of magnificent warships with powerful canons that were visiting what is now Singapore. The sultan visited Singapore and met Commodore James Brookes, British Navy. He convinced Brookes to come to Borneo and defeat the Ibans—the poison dart, blowpipe, head-hunter guys. Brookes easily defeated the Ibans. For his reward, the sultan gave Brookes what is today Sarawak. Brookes built a fortress named after his wife, Margarita; a governor's mansion; and British courthouse in Kuching, Sarawak. All buildings are in good condition and can be visited today.

8 & 9. A walk along the Riverfront is a great way to recharge your batteries, day or night.

10 & 11. Two views looking from the Riverfront across to Astana—the governor's mansion, built by James Brookes in 1840. A Chinese dragon, mythical symbol of masculinity, protects the Riverfront, while two Malay ladies chitchat.

12. A few sampans cross paths on their way to and from Astana.

13. Fort Margarita was also built by James Brookes in 1840 to protect Kuching. It is located across the river from the Riverfront, a few yards from Astana.

14. Above are peace fountains near the world-class Kuching museum.

15 & 16. The pagoda entrance to Kuching's Chinatown, with its many interesting shop houses; families live on the second floor and run their business on the ground floor. Malaysians drive on the left side of the street, but do everything else RIGHT!

17 & 18. Malaysians love their fruit. It's best to buy what they're selling today, green bananas cut from trees this morning.

19. They love their motorbikes too. A large percent of the population rides motorbikes.

20. A monument to the sampan river warriors is on display at the Riverfront.

21 & 22. Express boats—a fast-flying, fast-floating fuselage—are built in Kuching and sold to India, Papa New Guinea, Indonesia, Thailand, the Philippines, and China. Below is an express boat on its way to Sibu heading up the Rajang River. They reach speeds of forty knots.

23. A look at the interior of an express boat—two small seats on each side of the aisle.
24. An express boat arrives in Sibu. (below)

25 & 26. The Grand Mosque in Kuching, it takes on many different faces.

27. Famous India Street and the Grand Mosque. Buy two yards of colorful silk in one shop, have a tailor at another make you something special with a stylish Malaysian theme.

28. One of several Chinese temples in Kuching. A few joist sticks are burning to appease the gods.

29 & 30. There is no shortage of Chinese temples and Chinese architecture in Kuching.

31 & 32. Some have asked, "What's a typical home like in Kuching?" Best response, "You'll find lots of vegetation"—i.e., bamboo, orchids, fifty wild fruit trees, and your own homegrown favorite tea plants. We cannot drink enough tea to keep up with the plant growth, or eat all the fruits on the property, i.e., rambutan, papaya, banana, breadfruit.

33 & 34. Malaysia has four thousand wild orchids in the jungle, about thirty at Loon Woon's home. They bore some people because they bloom all year long.

35 & 36. Four thousand types of fungus grow too, and four million types of insects are always ready to bite.

37 & 38. If you love orchids, Malaysia is the place to visit.

39 & 40. Amazing, to think they grow outside with little care.

40 & 41. The best are grown in Sarawak, Borneo.

42 & 43. There are approximately twenty thousand natural orchid species and about ten thousand hybrids inbred by man.

44 & 45. No one knows if God is a Buddhist, Muslim, Jew, Hindu, Christian, or otherwise; but we all can agree that God is a creative genius, and he or she loves orchids. If we can agree on this simple principle, why can't we agree on another simple principle—stop the killing and live in peace.

46. Everyone's favorite.

47 & 48. It is impressive that so many varieties can all be found in one small garden.

49. An exotic flower.

50. A Venus flytrap plant is often an indoor decoration.

51. Chinese lanterns appear all over Kuching during Chinese New Year. Loon never puts his away. He celebrates all year long.

52. A yellow-vented bulbul feeds its chicks in a nest built of banana leaves in Loon's garden.

53. Glad to see someone is making good use of the banana leaves and enjoying the berries.

54. Good friend and warm, unpretentious, gentlemen, Loon Woon (nicknamed Loony Tunes, seated on the right) entertains his brother from Mainland China and his son, Wee Young, a distinguished mechanical engineer living in Singapore, who speaks excellent English, many dialects of Chinese, and Japanese. That's Wee Young's wireless computer on the table.

55. A typical traffic circle surrounded by cat statues in downtown Kuching.

Kuching, Malaysia at Night, a Photo Journal

1 & 2. In Malay, *merdeka* means *independence*. In 2007, Malaysia celebrated its fifty years of independence from the UK. Sidebar: There are fourteen stripes on the flag, but only thirteen states; the State of Singapore seceded from Malaysia to form its own country in 1961. Malaysia hasn't changed its flag. Perhaps Singapore will return someday.

3 & 4. Crown Plaza Hotel, Kuching.

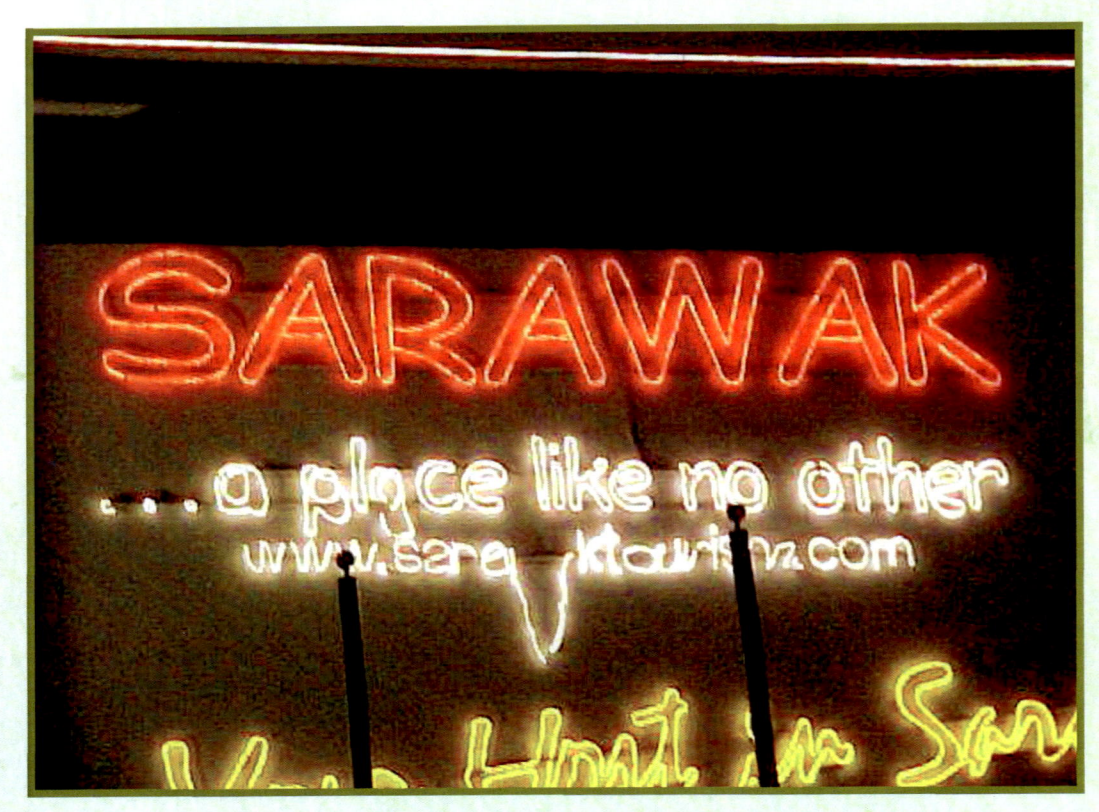

5 & 6. Sarawak River, Kuching—the Riverfront at sunset.

7 & 8. On his way to the hooch, sampans don't operate at night. The Buddhist Temple is always open.

9 & 10. Peace Garden waterfalls.

11. Fountain of Peace near the world-class Kuching museum.

12 & 13. Colorful streetlight pole decorations come in a dozen traditional Malaysian culture themes.

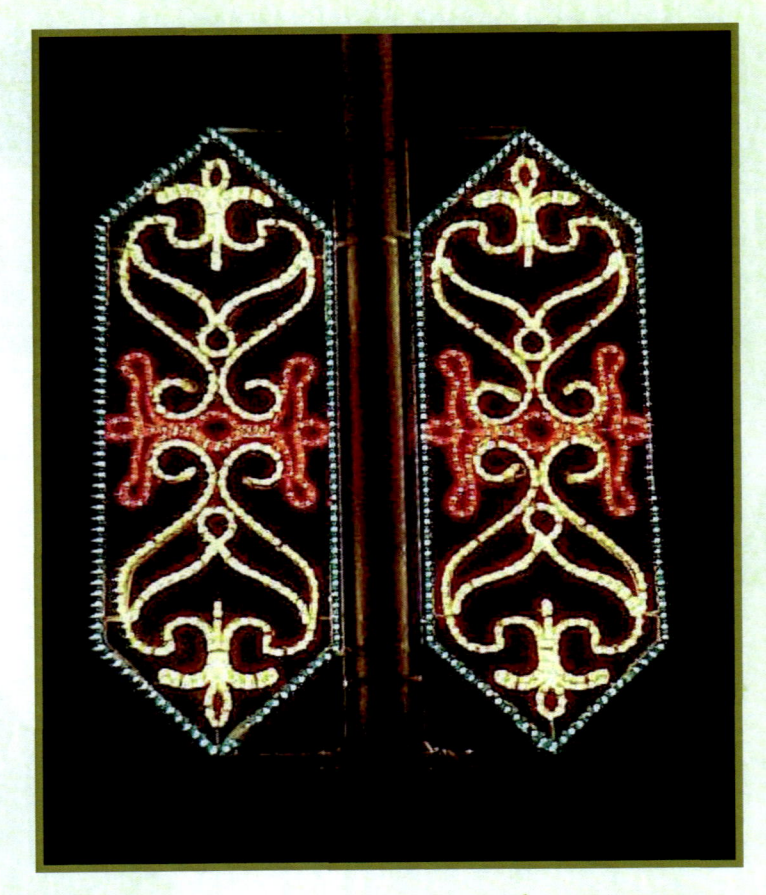

14 & 15. Warrior shields in an assortment of colors and patterns appear as decorations in Sarawak State buildings and hotels. Here they appear on streetlight poles.

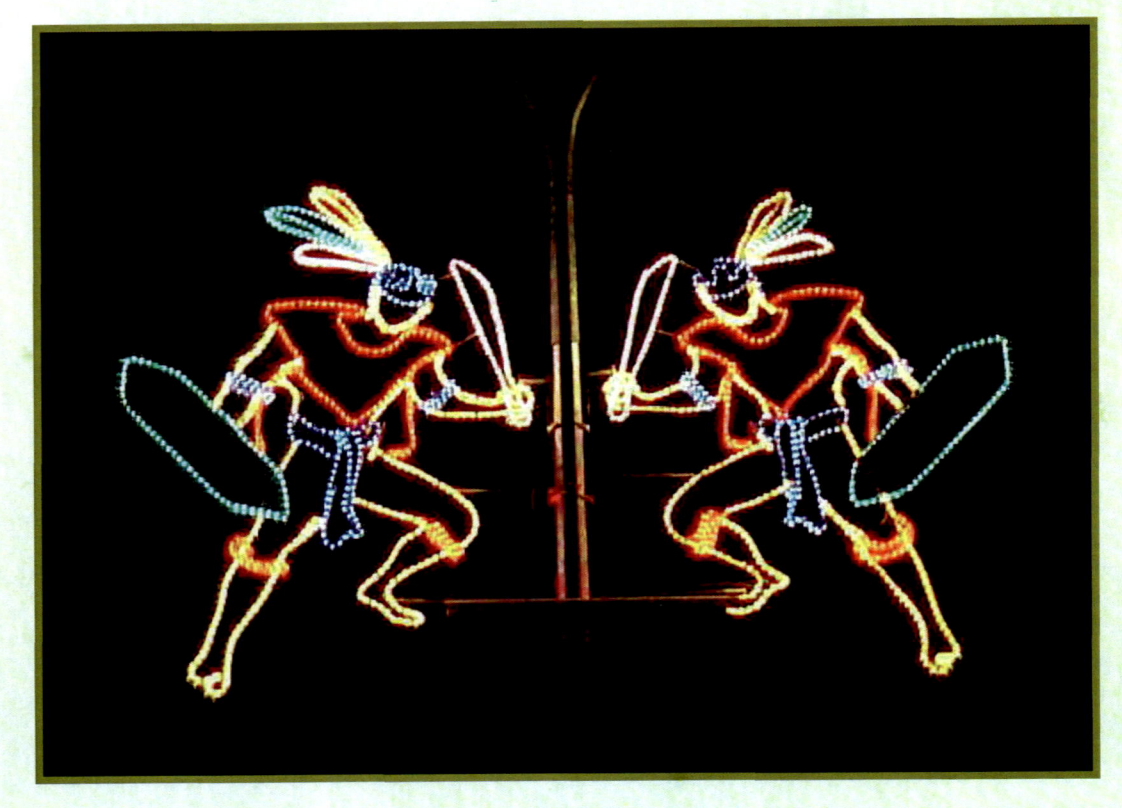

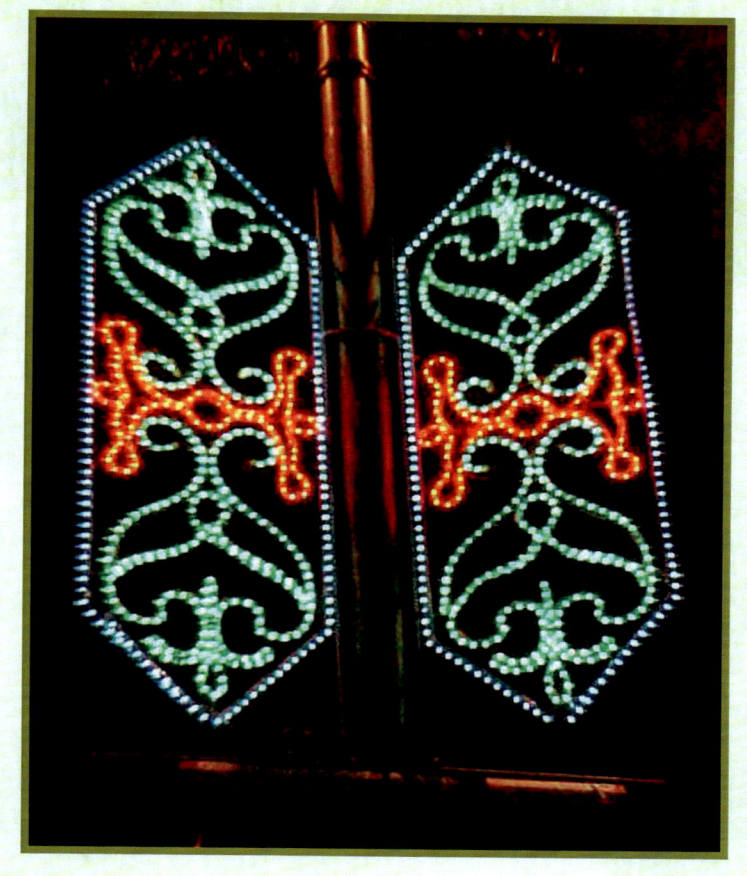

16 & 17 . More warrior shields and Malay ladies demonstrating a traditional native bird dance.

18. Iban warriors—the headhunter, poison dart, blow pipe guys that James Brooks help the sultan of Brunei defeat to win Sarawak.

19. Perhaps the best-known streetlight of them all.

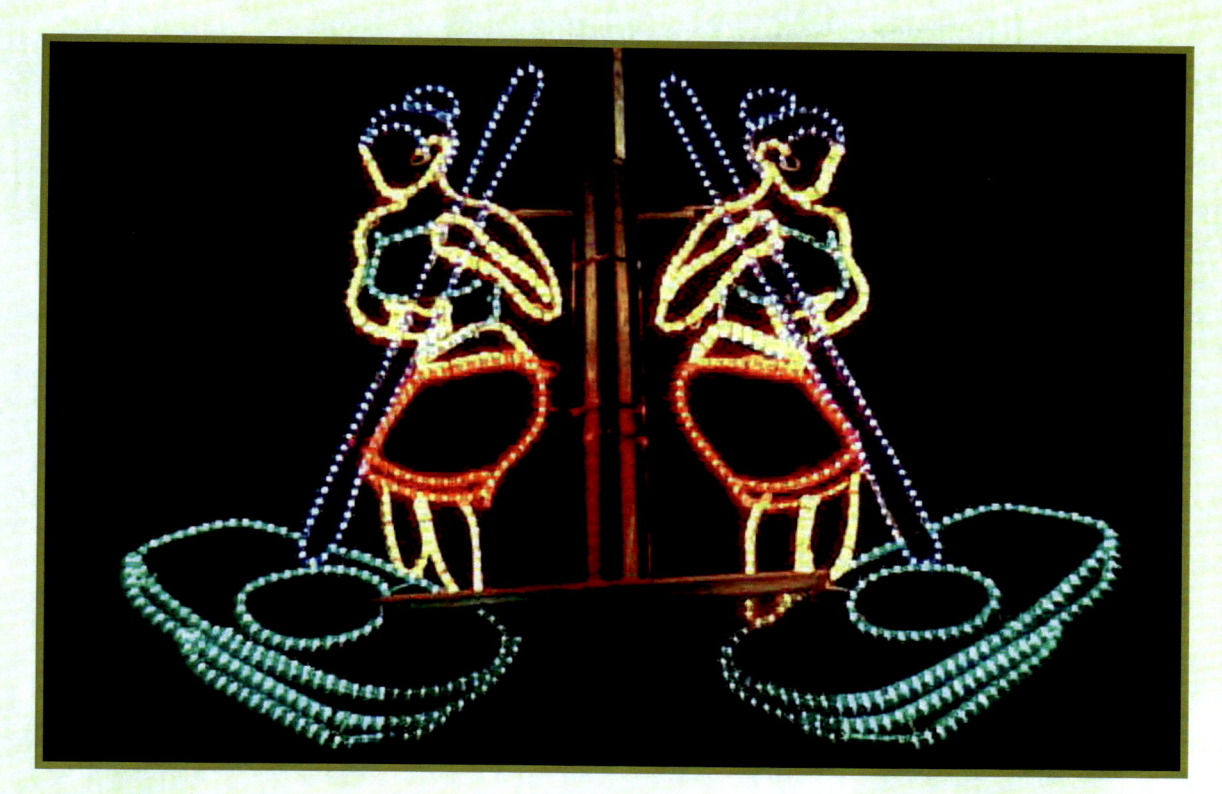

20. Malaysian ladies pound rice to remove the husk. Many tasks done by machine in the West are done by hand in some villages in the East.

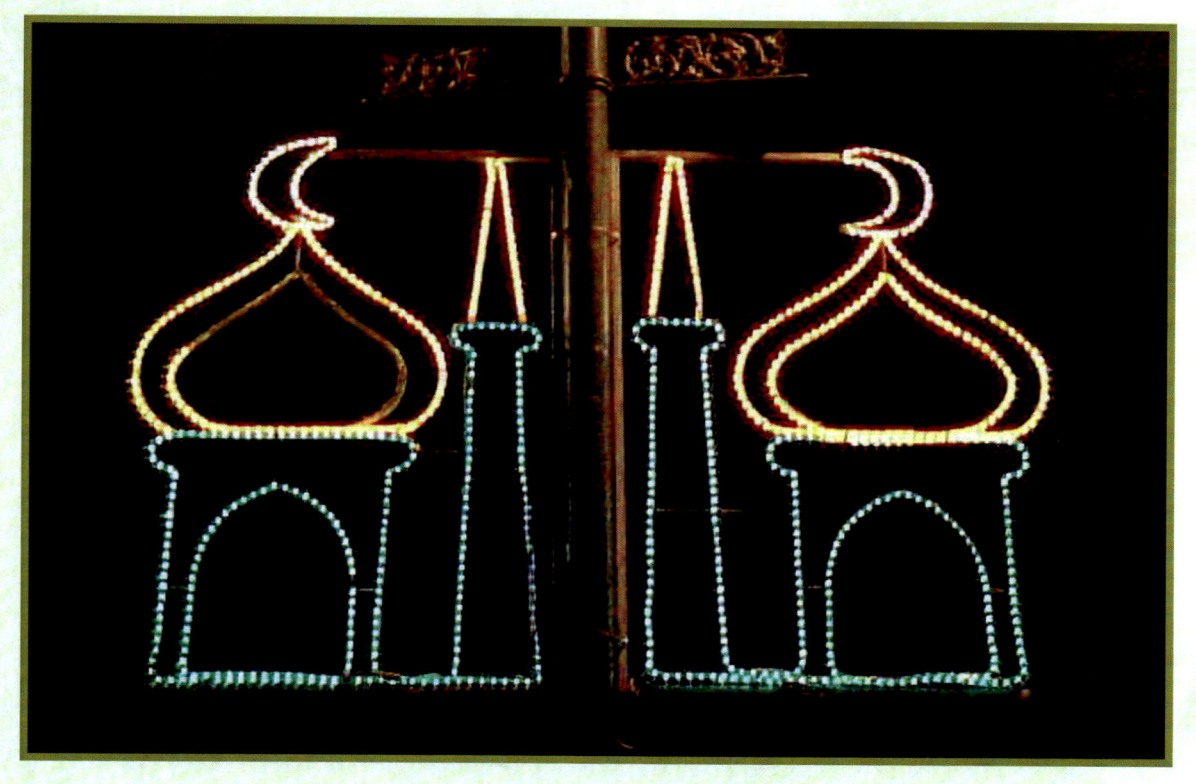

21. Muslim mosques are found everywhere in Sarawak.

22. A hilltop Chinese temple below.

23 & 24. Some orchids contrast better at night.

25 & 26. Nicknamed a couple of flying nuns waiting for a bus.

27. A water lily sits in Loon's pond, which is only one meter by one meter (three feet by three feet) built inside a truck tire. The camera can hide all sorts of unwanted detail.

28. In the daylight, you may walk past this orchid and hardly take notice, but it's striking at night.

29. One of Sarawak's rare endemic flowers the locals nicknamed the red olive plant.

30. From Kuching—the Cat City. That's all folks!

Malaysia – State of Sarawak, life beyond Kuching.

1 & 2 . A charming native lady dances the bird dance at the Cultural Village, thirty minutes from Kuching, with authentic hornbill feathers. Malaysia has eighteen species of hornbills.

3. A blowpipe gunner, he can drop a fly from fifteen yards.

4. A rhinoceros hornbill can be seen in the wild at many national parks in Sarawak. Some tribes have sustenance privilege, which grants them the right to hunt and gather in the parks. Hence, the villagers are sometimes seen wearing hornbill feathers. Ugh!

5. THE RAIN FOREST of BORNEO, a fine example of a tropical "cloud forest."

6. Which way is up? In many areas of the thick rain forest, small dugout canoes are the choice mode of transportation over the still, shallow streams.

7. A good view of the hot, humid cloud forest.

8. Two giant seahorses guard the harbor at Miri, Sarawak.

9. A 1850s relief of Malay carrying a kris tucked in his belt.
Knifes weren't just for show; they were everyday useful tools.

10. There are many species of lizards, including the seldom seen flying lizard in the jungles of Malaysia.

11 & 12. Cockfighting is still an entertainment to some native Malays.

13 & 14. Poison dart, blowpipe guys are not fans of hornbills.

15. An authentic working longhouse community. This tribal elder is repairing furniture.

16. Less than a century ago, young men wishing to marry must first prove their masculinity by bringing the head of an enemy tribesman to their perspective father-in-law. The practice was outlawed by the British, but put back into practice when the Japanese invaded Malay in 1941, provided the head was Japanese. Many young people today have abandoned the longhouse lifestyle in favor of city life, running water, flush toilets, cell phones, and the Internet.

17. This man collected a few Japanese trophies, seen in the background, when he was a young warrior. One for each wife.

18 & 19. Recognize anyone?

20 & 21. A contemporary longhouse, deep in the rain forest of Borneo. Pigs and chickens wonder freely underneath. The residents drop garbage through the floor, which the animals below devour. Everything is made from materials readily found in the jungle, e.g., banana leaves, rattan, bamboo.

22. Another native tribe's longhouse.
23. Local preferred mode of group transportation is the longboat.

24 & 25. Local ladies are seen gathering herbs, roots, wild fruits, etc. There are no less than fifty wild fruits growing in the jungle. Fruit is always available, and many entrepreneurs sell it at roadside stands.

26 A hardworking elder tribesman in search of food of all sorts, i.e., fish, plants, and fruit.

27. Life is physical in the rain forest. If you want to survive, you must work hard.

28. No fish caught this day.

29. One of two pools at Damai Beach Resort, which is thirty minutes from Kuching on the South China Sea.

30. Fabulous accommodations at Damai Beach Resort.
31. Photo below was taken from inside the waterfall. Turtle Island can be seen in the distance.

32 & 33. You won't go hungry in the rain forest, there's plenty of food in the wild. Slugs—try one. They're tasty and full of slimy protein. You say, "You'd starve to death first." Me too.

Batang AI National Park and Longhouse Resort Malaysia

1 & 2. Batang AI is a beautiful place to relax and enjoy nature. Billed by the Hilton as a "naturalist paradise," it is built on an island, on a man-made lake, deep in the heart of the rain forest. Bring a ball cap, sunblock, and mosquito repellent. Shown in the artist rendering are authentic longhouse and rhinoceros hornbill. You can book an excursion to an authentic longhouse and stay overnight with an Iban tribe—the headhunter, poison dart, and blowpipe guys.

3 & 4. Great pool—waters always warm. A few Europeans are enjoying themselves. It's interesting to note that most Malaysians, especially those of the Islamic Malay and Chinese cultures, do not like to be seen in a bathing suit in public. Consequently, the beautiful pools are seldom frequented.

5. Malaysia's population is about 60 percent Malay Muslims, 30 percent Chinese, and 10 percent Indian and others. The three cultures don't like to be seen in a bathing suit. That leaves the pool wide open for visitors.

6. Kim Ngo Foo, visiting from Washington, is enjoying her native country.

7 & 8. A trek through the rain forest in quest of birds. First, we climb to the top of the lower canopy of tress, ladders are helpful. Then we enter the Canopy Walkway, a suspension bridge reported to be made of strong rope, for a rewarding walk among the treetops to observe nature at close range.

9 & 10. Oh my, it doesn't look too steady. Those are aluminum ladders and wood planks tied together. Malaysia has a different safety standard than some countries. It may be a rewarding experience just to get across.

11 & 12. I'm kneeling because I am too scared to stand.
Picture is blurred because the walkway is swaying up and down, left and right.

13 & 14. Wow! There's a beautiful golden pheasant on the jungle floor.

15 & 16. Durian fruit hangs from the upper canopy, about two hundred feet off the jungle floor. Don't let one of these ten-pound spiked bowling balls drop on you. Inside are gooey, sticky yellow fruits that taste like vanilla custard, but smell like my old sneakers. If you can get past the smell, they taste great. They are so smelly that most hotels ban them. One advantage of the Canopy Walk is that you can help yourself to some fruit without waiting for it to drop on your head.

17. "Okay, Kenneth, from here we climb that rickety old wooden ladder, you can see above us, to the top of the upper dipterocarp canopy. Now that ladder isn't as strong or steady as this platform, so I want you to be extra careful"
"Well ghee, Zait, thanks for the heads-up."

18. "Kenneth, we're almost to the top. There's a storm moving in, so take your time, but hurry up." "Thanks again, Zait."

19 & 20. "We made it. Good job, Zait. I take a better picture than you do, Zait, what do you think?" "How shamelessly presumptuous, Kenneth. By the way, that's the Indonesian State of Kalimantan in the distance. You need a visa to go there, but if President Bush's last trip to Jakarta is any indication, I would stay out of Indonesia if I were American." "Ghee, thanks again, Zait."

21 & 22. The trip down isn't much easier or safer. Every so often you come across a missing plank. For every missing plank, there is a tourist somewhere with a brand-new cast and a broken leg.

23 & 24. Ghost trees—the dam created them when it flooded the area.

25. "One last bridge to cross and its boots on the ground. Not to worry, Kenneth, that bamboo is stronger than it looks." "Ghee, thanks again, Zait. What about the crocodiles down below. Have they been fed today?"

26 & 27. Back on the Batang AI National Park trail (above); African tulip tree bloom (below).

28 & 29. African tulip trees flower all year.

30 & 31. There's always such a crowd at the pool.

32 & 33. Back at the Longhouse Resort. From the outside it doesn't look like much.

34. Inside view of Longhouse Community Room where the tribe gathers for meals and work on projects together. It's made mostly of ironwood. Looks much nicer from the inside.

35. Each guest room is two stories; the upper mezzanine is exclusively a superb bedroom. Beautiful woodwork carvings decorate the interior. Well worth the $75 US per night, this includes a sumptuous Malay-cuisine breakfast.

36. That's what we looked like the day after we shared a bottle of *tuak*—local homemade rice wine—at the Hilton's Wong Irup Club. That's me on the right; I forgot her name, the one on the left. But, as you can see, she's much prettier than I in the daylight.
37. Local Malay Iban art below.

38. How to get home? Malays say, "The roads of Sarawak are its mighty rivers." I say, "For each mile forward, you float one mile sideway and one mile backward. And you're not real sure where you're at when you get there."

39. The daily rain forest rainstorm (below) is heading our way. And rainstorms on the equator are mean. My dog runs to the bathroom to hide and wraps himself around the toilet bowl. For different reasons, so do my brother and father on long boat trips across the Alaskan Gulf from Valdez to Sitka.

40. It rains every afternoon for about two hours during the six-month rainy season—November through April. The sudden darkness and heavy rain are not as frightening as the lightning and claps of thunder.

41. Malaysia—magnificent and mystical.
42. Did you hear about the houseplant that swallowed a guy? This is it.

43 & 44 . Pineapples and beetle nuts grow wild in Malaysia.

45. We couldn't get the locals to explain what they did with the fruit or nuts growing on this Elog palm. But they did explain the plastic bags (look closely) used to collect sap from the trunk; they make palm wine from it.

46. Ruth Kiew, in her new book *Palma Malaysia* says the fruits are edible. The platform, however, was constructed to collect the sap for wine making. You have to set your priorities straight; leave generations of fruit hanging there collect the sap.

47 & 48. It's a boat ride and jungle van trip of four hours to Kuching. Just for the record, I had to scream and cry, lay on the floor, and squirm like a worm before they let me drive the boat. The entire Batang AI National Park experience is secluded, exciting, and an exceptional adventure.

NATIONAL PARKS OF BORNEO MALAYSIA

1. Mulu National Park, Sarawak, Borneo, is a popular tourist attraction. A grueling three-day journey via longboat, jungle treks, river crossings, and steep climbs will take you to the top of the mountain in the background. From there you can view the rare, majestic limestone pinnacles, for which the park is famous.

2. Loony-Tune Woon, lifelong friend of the author, at the entrance to Mulu National Park.

3 & 4. Mulu National Park has four outstanding caves—Lang, Deer, Clearwater, and Wind caves.

5 & 6. Travel between the caves is by longboat. It is sometimes rough going, especially when the sandbars are encountered and all hands are asked to help carry the boat.

7 & 8. A trip to see the caves is best done by longboat, on rivers the color of a chocolate shake that snake east, then west, then east again, or two hours on foot with a guide by fording the river at a few narrow bends—your choice. You can visit all four caves in a single day via an enjoyable, sometimes exciting, longboat sojourn.

9. The entrance to Deer Cave. Two hundred stairs to climb—ugh!

10 & 11. A busy day at the caves.

12 & 13. Seen above is a ranger station and visitor center at one of four caves in Mulu National Park. A ranger is needed 24/7 to prevent theft of the swift nests. Bird's nest soup is a coveted delicacy. The portrait below is natural and *not* man-made. Any guess who it looks like? (Majority of visitors guess U.S. president Abraham Lincoln.)

14. He's got a good place to watch a million bats when they swarm from the cave at dusk. I'd wear a poop-repellent hat.

15. Here they come! About one million fruit bats leave the caves every day at dusk and swarm through the jungle, eating insects.

16. No matter what time of year or where you go, the rain forest is always thick and green.

17. Deer Cave has the largest cave entrance in the world and the most pungent scent of bat droppings—guano.

18. Mulu's majestic limestone pinnacles—a rough three-day trek and one-thousand-meter (3,328 feet) vertical climb. Not a trip for the fainthearted.

19. The adventure to the top of Gunung Api begins with a two-hour boat ride over rapids, followed by a four-hour trek through virgin rain forest, where you are expected to ford Melinau River twice. But not to worry, waist deep in rushing water, there is a wire rope to cling to. Overnight at Camp 5, a heavenly meadow with a lean-to, enjoy a home-cooked Malaysian-cuisine meal prepared by the park ranger and his lovely bride. It's up early for the strenuous one-thousand-meter ascent to the top. After viewing the spectacular pinnacles and enjoying a box lunch at the top, its back down, another night with the ranger and his wife, before heading back in the morning.

20. There are several hundred endemic species of dipterocarp trees in Borneo that make up the rain forest's upper canopy. This photo clearly demonstrates the change in elevation between the lower and upper canopy. The tualang or honey tree, reputed to be the tallest trees in Malaysia and third tallest in the world, is shown above. Pied hornbills and emerald doves like to feed on its fruit.

21 a, b, & c. Orangutan, meaning "man of the jungle," can easily be seen, up close and personal, at Semonggok Wildlife Sanctuary or the Mutang Wildlife Sanctuary near Kuching, and the Sepilok Orang Utan Rehabilitation Center near Sandakan, Sabah.

22. Be prepared for anything on the hiking trails of Borneo.

23. Green Viper—a good creature to avoid.

24. Rafflesia flowers can be seen all year long in bloom at Gunung Gading National Park. This magnificent flower, reputed to be the world's largest, measures about one meter (three feet) in full bloom. I think they're ugly. They don't smell pretty either. I haven't tasted one yet.

25. Carnivorous pitcher plants come in all assortments of shapes and sizes. They are found throughout the rain forests of Borneo.

26. There are plenty of vines for Tarzan and Jane, and monkeys to swing from.
Fig vines have been known to strangle to death two hundred feet (thirty-eight meters) kapok trees.

27. Carnivorous pitcher plants come in a variety of colors, shapes, and sizes.

28. Malaysia's much-loved fan palm.

29 & 30. Mount Kinabalu National Park's highest peak is at 13,450 feet (4,100 meters) is the highest mountain in Southeast Asia. It takes two strenuous days of hiking to climb to the top and back. Plan on climbing to about eleven thousand feet the first day and stay at the bulk-bed "halfway house." Awakened at 1:30 a.m., the trek continues to the top by torchlight. Expect to reach the top in time to witness a spectacular sunrise.

31. Time to board a longboat for what might be a treacherous thirty-minute ride across the open waters of the South China Sea to Bako National Park. The jetty looks none too safe either. Be careful, in 1994 my father fell off.

32. Malaysian's prefer to live in stilt houses built over bay or harbor water.

33. Bako National Park is rated among the world's top ten best national parks by the author.

133

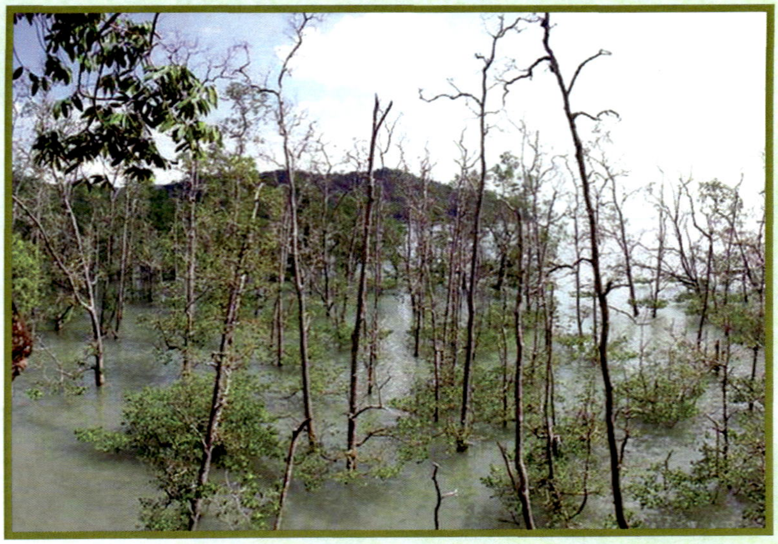

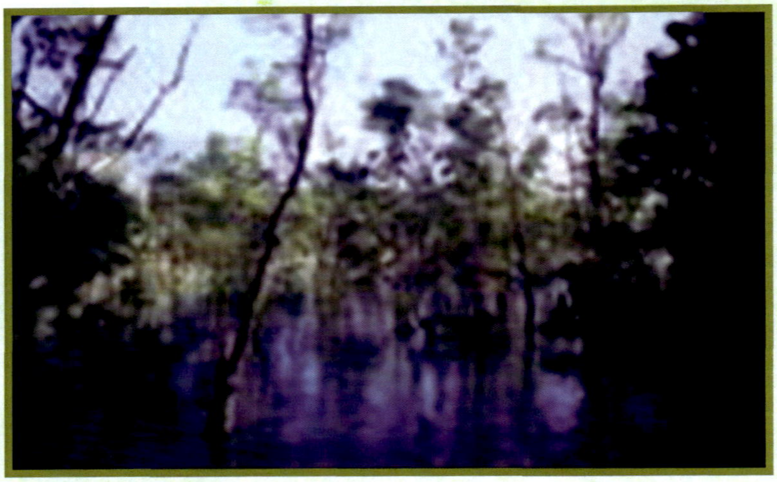

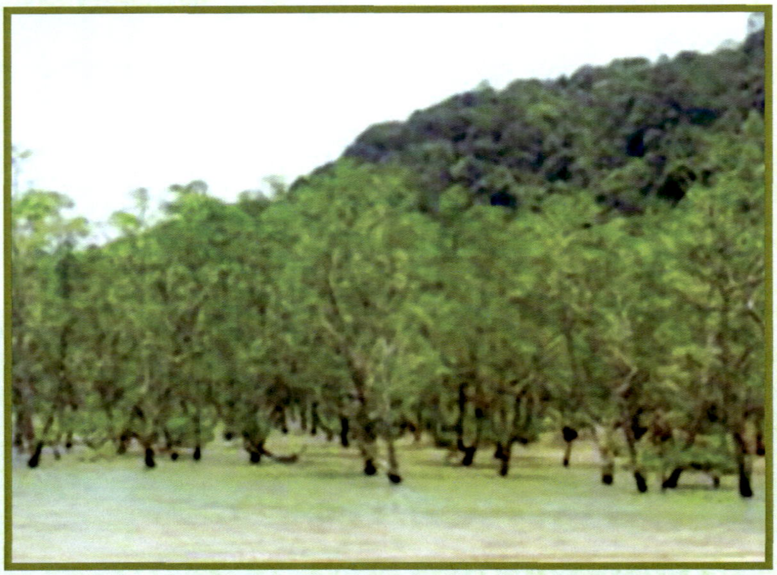

37. The ever-changing face of Bako mangrove. A plank walk allows visitors to explore the mangrove in search of the four hundred species of migratory and native birds, and dozen mammals.

38. Shown are the silver-leaf monkeys. They are gentle and tame. Keep your distance from the long-tailed macaque monkeys; besides being thieves, they can be nasty, fierce, and vicious.

39 & 40. You will see wild boar, locally known as the bearded pig. They like to "cut the grass" at the canteen.

41. One of several sea stacks created by sea spray, wave action, and wind.

42 & 43. Two of the beautiful enchanted and secluded beaches on the far side of the park. It takes about two hours to hike over the top of Bako Mountain and down the other side to reach these pristine beaches, but well worth the effort. Because of the uphill, strenuous climb, in the heat of the equator, few people make the trek, leaving the beaches secluded and enchanting.

45. Bako NP's enchanted coves invite you!
The author can help arrange a guest cabin at Bako NP by contacting him via e-mail: Kbrophy@msn.com.
Come for a visit.

46. Sunset over the South China Sea.

47. Taken from the Visitor Center area at Bako NP beach. Damai Beach is in the distance.

48. A golden estuary, where freshwater meets the sea.

49 & 50. In Sarawak, the pace is light, travel by boat primitive, food simple but spicy, people genuine and friendly, sunsets stunning, and the overall adventure is outstanding.

Peninsular Malaysia

1 & 2. There are several hundred birds of prey circling overhead. They are land birds that just migrated down from China, on their way to warmer climate. To avoid the harsh winter of the Northern Hemisphere, they fly thousands of miles to Indonesia's archipelago, south of the equator. They followed the coastline until they arrived here (see pointer) at Tanjung Piai National Park—the southernmost tip of mainland Asia. The young and inexperienced birds are circling to build up enough courage to cross such a large open body of water. Their first-ever such attempt. Or, they think I am over-the-hill and easy prey, as did the *mistaken* mountain lion that attacked the seventy-year-old man at Redwoods Park, California. He and his wife defended themselves with a ballpoint pen. I always carry a pen; these birds are in for a fight. The low black clouds in the distance are directly over Singapore. That could be another reason the birds are staying where they are.

141

3. Misbehave here and you walk boardwalk X. Be careful, it can get fogy at a mangrove. On a clear day, one can see Singapore. The ships shown are waiting in the Straits of Malacca to be off-loaded in Singapore. It is reported, they pay $5,000 per night to the Singaporean Coast Guard, for what amounts to official protection money, while they wait their turn to off-load. Ninety-nine ships were pirated last year in the Malacca Strait. My friend's father, ship, captain, and crew disappeared in 2004. No trace of them has ever been found; hundreds of similar cases remain unresolved.

Did you know?
- Sixty-three thousand ships carrying 30 percent of the world's trade and 50 percent of the world's oil passed through the Malacca Strait in 2007, making it the world's busiest shipping lane.
- Oil from the Middle East, on its way to America, passes so close to Tanjung Piai National Park that you can wave to the captain. Ugh!
- If you walk your way south from China, you will eventually arrive at Tanjung Piai NP, but a few years older.
- Tanjung Piai is a Ramsar site. For those who don't know, in 1974—while America was busy dealing with Arab oil embargos, the Vietnam War, and Nixon tapes—Turkey invaded Cyprus, and Iran held a wetlands conservation convention in the city of Ramsar, Iran. Many countries attended—America did not—and a *List of Wetlands of International Importance* was agreed upon. Once on the Ramsar list, the convention requires the country responsible "to take all steps necessary to ensure the maintenance of the ecological character of the site." There are fifty-three Ramsar sites. Malaysia has four Ramsar sites; the other three are the following: Pulau Kukup, Sungai Pulai, and Tasek Bera.

4. It is not far from Thailand, Myanmar, Cambodia, or Vietnam.

5. "New York—6,422 kilometers from Singapore . . . ." I don't think so.
I know a few pilots (Amelia Earheart, for example) and sea captains that wish that were true.

6. Tanjung Piai National Park Lodge and employees' stilt housing.
Many Malaysians prefer to live over water than on land.

7. Photographer Kim Ngo Foo; her friend, Andy; and our guide, Zait at the entrance to Endau-Rompin National Park.

8. Endau-Rompin is the most remote national park in Peninsula Malaysia. Coke is everywhere on the planet—no doubt they are on the moon. Andy is proud of a bag of wood chips that a native sold (swindled) him. Natives believe, if chewed, the chips increase male stamina—if you catch my drift. Andy has been chewing them all week. No progress reports yet.

9. The accommodation at Endau-Rompin National Park is affordable and comfortable. The journey here is rough.

10. An unknown and unusual flower. Most likely, you will see thousands of flowers and insects you have never seen before when visiting Malaysia.

11. Malaysia obtained its independence from Britain in 1957; the year 2007 marked its fifty years of nationhood.

12. Early morning finds us loading up the longboat for a trip up the Endau River.

13 & 14. Andy, never without his cell phone which worked fine in the park, enjoys the longboat ride up the Endau River.

15 & 16. Zait keeps an eye out for crocodiles, but mostly for shallow water and sandbars. Be prepared to help carry the boat across the sandbars.

16 & 17 . Expect rain every afternoon and be surprised if it doesn't.

18. The longboat skims along the surface at about twenty knots.

19. Thick, low bushy virgin forest lie alongside the banks of the Endau River.

20 & 21. The longboat departure challenge begins. It's tough trekking through a rain forest.

22 & 23. Time for some jungle trekking. Watch out for leeches. They love to suck blood. This is a trail cut through the jungle by day-to-day Asian elephant traffic. Let's hope we hear them, before we see them. There is elephant dung everywhere, so watch your step. These are new bamboo shoots. Tigers and sloth bears love to nibble on them. Close-up the ranks, there is strength in numbers. And get your ballpoint pens out and ready.

24. We're through the low bushy brush and now entering a cloud forest. Everything is always damp and constant temperature—just the way snakes, lizards, spiders, and leeches like it.

25 & 26. Flying buttress roots on a dipterocarp tree. Centuries old, this tree is about twenty-five feet (eight meters) in diameter.

27 & 28. No branches until about thirty feet (ten meters) up. Great sunsets too.

29. Perhaps the largest bird statue in the world; a brahminy kite is honored at Langkawi Island, twenty miles off the coast of Peninsular Malaysia. Its wingtip is about fifty feet (fifteen meters) off the ground. Every day at noon, the park service feeds hundreds along the Rhu River. The kites sweep down and snatch chicken parts off the water surface, making for great photo ops.

30. The Langkawi atolls are some of the least-populated and beautiful tropical islands in the world.

31. The Rhu River as it enters the Indian Ocean.

32. Amphibian "creepy" mud skimmers are common throughout Malaysia. Part fish, part snake, part snail, they give me the willies.
33. Something green tries to cover every inch of surface in Malaysia (below); solid rock cliffs are no exception.

33 & 34. Warm, clear turquoise water and breathtaking scenery makes Langkawi a special place.

35. Be sure to stop over in Kuala Lumpur (known to the locals as KL) when visiting Malaysia. Not only home to the world's tallest twin towers, the Petronas Towers, but also some great shopping, orchard and butterfly gardens, a zoo, and many other great attractions.

36. "Nice shirt you got there, Kenneth. Peru's my home country. Any chance you can get me back there?" "I'll see what I can do, Mr. Macaw." My blue-and-yellow macaw buddy and I hope you enjoyed this tour of Malaysia.

Seldom Seen Sights of the
PHILIPPINES

7,107 islands of sun, sand, and surf
to enjoy as evidenced by the laid-back
bamboo beach huts at Boracay.

A Snapshot of the Philippines

Dominated by over seven thousand islands, with some 60 percent uninhabited and many strung with low-elevation mountain ranges, poking through lush rain forests, dotted with fertile valleys (some covered in rice paddies and others curved in vivid green terrace farms), bordered by lovely beaches and an emerald green ocean—the Philippines is one of the loveliest places on earth and a magnet for all those who crave the great outdoors. Every imaginable outdoor activity from simple hiking the rain forest, beachcombing for seashells, sunbathing, bodysurfing, and snorkeling, to more equipment-intense scuba diving, sailing, and deep-sea fishing are available at the thousands of pristine seashore resorts located throughout the Philippines. Throughout the country, you will find friendly, hospitable people accustomed to a rustic lifestyle and living with less. They may appear to lead a simple lifestyle; but they are hardworking, elegant, gracious, and charming hosts. It is the only predominantly Roman Catholic country in Asia.

The Philippines is divided into four major groups of islands. Luzon in the north is the biggest island (141,395 square kilometers). Visayas, in the middle of the country, comprises a group of islands with about 56,606 square kilometers. Mindanao, in the south, is approximately 101,000 square kilometers. To the west, Palawan island is a favorite among tourist.

Boracay island is another wonderfully exciting island to visit. It has a world-class boardwalk that stretches for a few kilometers and offers quality restaurants, shopping, pubs, and live entertainment. You will find Boracay surrounded by beautiful sandy beaches with all manner of water sports including parasailing, Jet Skies, catamarans, wind and kite surfing, etc.

The Economy

The economy of the Philippines is as intricate as its islands are numerous. Filipinos are rightfully nicknamed the workers of the world. Filipinos sign contracts by the millions each year to live and work in foreign countries such as Iran, Iraq, Afghanistan, Saudi Arabia, Kuwait, etc., and hold down all manner of professional and blue-collar jobs as nurses, engineers, construction workers, bodyguards, bankers, janitors, etc. FACT: there are more expatriate Filipinos with legitimate work permits living and working day to day in Dubai, UAE, than there are natural-born UAE residents living in Dubai. For the most part, each expat Filipino is furnished housing and meals in the host country and sends his or her paycheck home to his or her family in the Philippines, thus fueling the Philippine's economy with much-needed international funds.

Within the Philippines, the economy is driven by banking, construction, manufacturing, agriculture, fishing, and transportation sectors. The thriving economy of the resort islands such as Palawan island and Boracay island are powered mainly by tourism. A combination of beautiful beaches, calm tide, excellent deep-sea fishing, comfortable yet affordable hotels, and excellent fresh seafood restaurants make the resort islands an excellent value. Korean and Japanese tourists flock to Boracay island by the hundreds of thousands to celebrate their national holidays.

Manila

The Philippines's most heavily populated area is the metropolis of Manila. Due to its five million people, heavy air pollution and traffic-congestion problems, gambling casinos, topless-bottomless girlie bars and prostitution, Manila is not a favorite place of this author. Since most international flights to the Philippines arrive in Manila, however, it is therefore a necessary stopover. Manila has a dozen major suburbs, such as the upscale Ortigas Center, the newest business and commercial hub of Manila with the excellent Holiday Inn Galleria Manila towering atop one of the most extraordinary, complex and world's grandest shopping malls, and other fine hotels and restaurants.

The Rain forests

Rainforest Tarsier

Few small countries on earth can rival the Philippines's biodiversity of flora and fauna. Besides beautiful beaches, the nation's coasts are often cloaked in lowland rain forests with complex ecosystems that harbor most of the country's wildlife. The cloud rat, Philippine crocodile, Philippine tarsier, and Mindoro dwarf buffalo are some of the wildlife that inhabit the understory, while exotic birds, monkeys such as the flying lemur and golden mantled fruit bats cavort in the upper canopy treetops. Rain forests often stretch from the coast to lower mountain slopes all the way to cloud-draped mountaintops, forming an uninterrupted sea of greenery. Bird and animal life is abundant with an exceptional array of biological diversity. A single half-kilometer plot of land in the Philippines lowland dipterocarp rain forest may well contain more than five hundred different species of trees, plants, ferns, and vines—a stunning degree of variety that pales, however, in comparison to the profusion and diversity of flowers, birds, and insects.

Will the rain forest be here in twenty-five years? Many scientists believe not. The Philippines are being plundered by greedy timber tycoons at an alarming rate. Unless something is done soon, the land will be denuded, and you can say good-bye to all those fine animals mentioned above as well as an additional four thousand species of endemic—found only in the Philippines—butterflies, birds, ferns, trees, mosses, and insects.

Natural Parks, National Parks, Wildlife Sanctuaries, and Wonders

In order to safeguard its precious natural heritage, the Philippines have set aside over a dozen areas as natural parks and wildlife sanctuaries. Together with natural forest management, conservation of wildlife, birds and marine life, nature reserves have been established through a network of protected areas. Almost one million acres of conservation areas are now protected. Some of the Philippines most popular natural and national parks, wildlife sanctuaries, and other protected areas are briefly discussed below.

A Philippine Eagle

Mount Apo Natural Park—Mt. Apo National Park, in Mindanao, is a dormant volcano and the Philippines's highest mountain (2,954 meters). Its habitat is a last stronghold of the national bird, the Philippine eagle. Apo's forested slopes are protected for the conservation of this endangered bird. The nonprofit Philippine Eagle Foundation (www.philippineeagle.org) has been specifically created to promote the survival of the rapidly vanishing Philippine eagle. Check out the site and learn how you can adopt an eagle. One of the rarest, largest, and most powerful birds in the world, its eagle's head is adorned with long brown feathers that give it the appearance of a lion's mane. This bird of prey, or raptor, is nicknamed bird king.

Puerto Princesa Subterranean River National Park—Located in Palawan Province, it features spectacular limestone karsts landscape country and an underground river, which is accessible by boat for tourism. The subterranean caverns are lit in beautiful red, blue, purple, green, and yellow lights. Night tours are ideal. One of the distinguishing features is that it emerges directly into the sea with its lower portion, thereby subject to tidal influences.

Tubbataha Reef Marine Park—This is located in the middle of the central Sulu Sea, 181 kilometers southeast of Puerto Princesa City, Palawan island. Day-tour boats take scuba divers and snorkelers. Covering 33,200 hectares, the park comprises two atolls, North and South Reefs, separated by an eight kilometer channel. The North Reef is a large oblong-shaped continuous reef platform two kilometers wide and completely enclosing a sandy lagoon some twenty-four meters deep. The most prominent feature is the North Islet, which serves as a nesting site for birds and marine turtles. Steep and often perpendicular walls extending to a depth of forty to fifty meters characterize the seaward face of the reef. Approximately four hundred species of colorful tropical fish have been recorded there. The coral is equally as colorful and diverse with species representing forty-six genera. The South Reef is a small triangular-shaped reef about one to two kilometers wide.

Chocolate Hills National Geological Monument—The Chocolate Hills range in elevation from one hundred meters to five hundred meters above sea level. The hills have been declared the National Geological Monument in recognition of its scientific value and geomorphic uniqueness. The conical, almost perfectly symmetrical shape, and relative size is among all the hills. They received the nickname Chocolate Hills because during the dry season, when precipitation is inadequate, the grass-covered hills turn chocolate brown. The hills are located throughout the towns of Carmen, Batuan, and Sagbayan and consist of 1,776 mounds (doesn't that number sound familiar?) of the same general shape.

Turtle Islands Wildlife Sanctuary—It is part of the Sulu archipelago, which is composed of approximately four hundred islands of varying shapes and sizes. It is located at the southwestern tip of the Philippines, about one thousand kilometers southwest of Manila. Turtle Islands are right at the edge of the international treaty limits separating the Philippines and Malaysia. The group of islands is situated south of Palawan and northeast of Sabah, Malaysia. The smallest island, the Langaan, measures about 7 hectares, while the largest, the Taganak Island, is about 116 hectares. It was proclaimed a wildlife sanctuary by memorandum of agreement between the Republic of the Philippines and the government of Malaysia, which declared Turtle Islands a heritage protected area. Turtle Islands WS is regarded as a major nesting ground with more than one thousand green turtle nesters annually. There are only ten remaining nesting sites worldwide. The hawksbill turtle also nests here but in smaller numbers. Worldwide, marine turtle populations have critically declined; hence, the United Nations has declared all species of marine turtle endangered.

El Nido–Taytay Managed Resource Protected Area—It is located on the northwestern tip of the mainland of Palawan. In 1991, the government of the Philippines proclaimed Bacuit Bay a marine reserve. It is now known as El Nido–Taytay Managed Resource Protected Area, which covers over thirty-six thousand hectares of land and fifty-four thousand hectares of marine waters. It contains towering limestone cliffs, beaches, mangroves, clear waters, unique forests, and limestone pinnacles. It is home to five species of mammals, including the Malayan pangolin and sixteen bird species endemic to Palawan including the threatened Palawan peacock pheasant, the Palawan hornbill, and Palawan scoops owl. Bacuit Bay is also home to the dugong dolphins and marine turtles, many of which are threatened species. Colorful coral reef fishes are found here. Some of the better known are butterfly fish, parrot fish, wrasses, trigger fish, angelfish, surgeon fish, damsel fish, emperors, snappers, groupers, and rabbit fish.

Banaue Rice Terraces—The mountain rice terraces at Banaue, Ifugao Province, Cordillera region, Luzon island in north Central Luzon are a world heritage site inscribed by UNESCO in 1995, and are sometimes referred to as the "eighth wonder of the world." The terraces were built over two thousand years ago for rice production by the Ifugao tribes, who first migrated to the Philippines from Taiwan. They are renowned in that for two thousand years, they have successfully contoured the mountains in harmony between humankind and the environment. The terraces are situated one thousand five hundred meters above sea level (five thousand feet) and cover an area of approximately ten thousand square kilometers (four thousand square miles).

PHILIPPINES

1. One of 7,101 Filipino islands, Boracay is first choice of many. If you like diving, snorkeling, bodysurfing, sailing, and sand sculpture, then Boracay island is the place for you. Talented local artists are paid to create a unique sculpture every day. In the evenings, the skies tend to get a tint of purple.

2. Outrigger-equipped sailboats, such as the *Boxer*, can be had for as little as $100 per day including a crew of three. With fair winds, you can circle Boracay island in four to six hours—A MAGNIFICENT SOJOURN!

3. One of the crew of three, whom the author envied the most.
Standing in the salty air breeze to counterbalance the catamaran looks like fun.

4. One of the 65 percent of the 7,101 islands that is uninhabited.

5. My toes are evidence that I attended this thrilling, exciting, adventurous, wave-running sojourn around Boracay island.

6. The captain salutes the customer. We began at noon, expected back by 5:00 or 6:00 p.m., arrived in the dark at 9:00 p.m. No lights on the *Boxer*, UGH! Winds are sometimes unpredictable.

7. If you like the thrill of sailing without the complexity and responsibility of owning your own yacht, the Philippines is the place for you.

8. Plenty of boats, lots of negotiating room.
You can barter in the Philippines.

9. Walk the plank and board the boat to begin a fine adventure. It may look like a strange insect, but it is actually a fine system of outriggers that keep the boat upright while traveling at high speed over rough seas.

10. Mysterious coral reefs at Tubbataha Reef Marine NP conceal all manner of colorful, unusual, intriguing fish and mollusks.

11. Remarkable volcano cauldrons and crater lakes exist throughout the Philippines. They are protected by the Filipino National Park Service. Take a helicopter tour and see this beautiful Pinatubo crater at Pampanga for yourself.

12. It can be lonely on these isolated islands. According to *Wikipedia: The Free Encyclopedia*, 4,327 islands are unnamed, and many of these are uninhabited.

13. The water is so crystal clear and clean, we were hesitant to jump in and spoil it.

14. Filipinos play hard and healthy, and they work hard and healthy.

15. Farmer and wife working their terrace rice plot—hard and grueling work.

16 & 17. Bagco Rice Terraces have been admired for symmetry and purpose for centuries.

18. There are loads of inexpensive high-speed water sport opportunities throughout the Philippines.

19. Chocolate Hills National Geological Park has unique rolling hills that look like candy gumdrops.

20. The summit of Mt. Pulag National Park is covered with grass and dwarf bamboo plants. At lower elevations, the mountainside has a mossy forest veiled with fog, and full of ferns, lichens, and moss.

21. The Philippines must import all of its oil; thus, thrifty Filipinos on Palawan island ride motorcycles or take tricycle taxis.

22. Crowded villages on stilts (stilt village) over the water are preferred housing to many poor families on Palawan island.

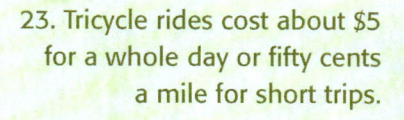

23. Tricycle rides cost about $5 for a whole day or fifty cents a mile for short trips.

24. El Nido–Taytay Protected Area is located on the northwest tip of Palawan island. It is so important to protect such treasures. Without strong conservation and protectionist organizations, this area of Palawan island would soon look like the stilt village noted above.

25. Friends are easy to make in the Philippines. This is Honda Bay on Palawan island.

Seldom Seen Sights of
CHINA

Above: China is the last stronghold of the endangered panda. China is the only country in the world where the panda roams freely in the wild.

A Snapshot of China

Enter China, land of chopsticks, dim sum, tea, pandas and tigers, silk robes and slippers, Shangri-La, red flags with crescent moons, bicycles and more bicycles, Mount Everest, Tibet, puppet shows, mysterious temples, sumptuous delicacies, exotic architecture, and the smells of incense, coal pollution, and frying spice.

China is the world's fourth largest country (after Russia, Canada, and the USA); it has, however, the world's largest and fast-growing population at approximately 1.4 billion people (as of July 2007). Its massive population, and somewhat overcrowded conditions, is perhaps the first thing that strikes most visitors to China. You may find yourself wondering, "How do they do it? Where does the food and water in such abundant quantity come from? How does the government control supply and demand, and care for so many people?" Although the Chinese militaristic form of government imposes strict controls over everyday life and has its share of negative press—runaway pollution, imprisonment of innocent political dissidents, Tibetan imperialism, minority discrimination and women's rights issues, exploitation of African nations, etc.—the government deserves some credit for keeping the chopsticks chopping; there is relatively low unemployment, a chicken in every pot, and for much of the population, living standards have improved dramatically in the past few years. In fact, it is reported that there are more self-made millionaires in China than anywhere else in the world. In this regard, the Chinese government deserves a lot of credit. Some reports indicate the population increases by over a million people a month, that's the size of an average city anywhere else in the world. For that reason, it's safe to say, China's population increases by a new city each month. No wonder China has plans under way to build ten new nuclear power plants, each year, for the next ten years—one hundred new nuclear power plants are either on the drawing boards or in the field under construction. Wow, now that's an impressive statistic!

Mostly mountains, high plateaus, deserts in the west, plains in the east, deltas, hills, lakes, wetlands, snaking gargantuan rivers—you name it, and China's vast terrain has it somewhere. With so much to offer, not to worry, your trip to China will be a unique adventure. Mount Everest on China's border with Nepal is the world's tallest peak and one such unique adventure that awaits you. Something a little more down to earth (pardon the pun) is a relaxing journey to Lijiang Old Town in . . . Providence at the foot of Jade Dragon Snow Mountain National Park. With thirteen snaking mountain peaks, all over fifteen thousand feet, spread out to resemble the back of a dragon, Jade Dragon Snow Mountain NP is aptly named. A picturesque ride to the top aboard the world's highest and longest cable car drops you at fifteen thousand feet. You can purchase a bottle of oxygen or rough it to the top. A wooden boardwalk snakes to the farthest point up, where a cameraman is waiting to take your momentous picture. Be sure to get down in time to catch what many consider the finest theater production in China, the Lijiang Impressions. Inside an open-air amphitheater at the bottom of the mountain, but inside the national park, a cast of a one thousand performs Chinese tribal song and dance numbers that are fabulous. Also, don't miss the charming Chinese culture performance at the village theatre in Old Town.

A Glimpse at China's History

If it's true the *past informs the present*, then China, with its ten-thousand-year history, has a most informed modern-day society. First evidence of primitive agricultural settlements date back to 8000 BC found along the eastern coastal regions and the fertile deltas of the Yellow and the Yangzi rivers. The headwaters of the Yangzi are home to Tiger Leaping Gorge National Park (see photos herein)—the third largest gorge in the world behind the Grand Canyon, USA, and an unnamed gorge in Tibet, China. Civilizations along the rivers flourished by cultivating rice and fishing. Not too much different from the core values of society in many rural areas of China today. Broken earthenware and black ceramics, found by archeologist, tell little about the history of China for the first six thousand years. China was first ruled by emperors in 1600 BC with the birth of the Shang dynasty. Dynasty power centered on the emperor whose authority was divine and thought to be mandated from heaven. It was believed that the emperor could communicate with God and his ancestors, wherever they may be. The period of emperors lasted from 1600 BC until AD 1911 and was marked by fighting between rival factions, periods of peace and prosperity, conquest by Genghis Khan global isolation, and limited trading *with the West*. Greed and corruption, dereliction of duty, gluttony, inbreeding, and self-indulgence (keeping a harem of two thousand concubines) are some of the reasons that caused one dynasty to collapse and another ambitious new empire to deliver. A summary of the history and important contributions of significant dynasties follows:

- **Shang Dynasty (1600–1050 BC)**—The beginning of China's Bronze Age and the start of the palace culture. First evidence of Chinese writing dating back to 1294 BC.
- **Zhou Dynasty (1050–221 BC)**—Established China's capitol in Xi'an. Long periods of constant warfare. Feudal warlords sacked the capital and killed the emperor.
- **Qin, Han, and Miscellaneous Dynasties (221 BC–AD 581)**—China divided into warring parties setting up a Southern Dynasty with its capital in Nanjing, and a Northern Dynasty with its capital in Datong and Luoyang. Standardized a system of money. Conscripted millions of slaves to build the Great Wall to divide the North from the South. (History is thankful that Abraham Lincoln did not have the same idea.)
- **Sui Dynasty (581–AD 618)**—United China. Built the Grand Canal and a flotilla of ships, many consider China's first navy.
- **Tang Dynasty (618–AD 907)**—Thought of as the golden age of China and characterized by prosperity and social development. Trade flourished by land and sea. Territorial expansion usurped Korea, Vietnam, and southern Siberia, increasing China to its largest size in its history. Buddhism spread like wildfire. Silk paintings gained popularity.
- **Song Dynasty (960– AD1279)**—Built urban centers, communication systems, and stimulated economic development.
- **Mongol Rule (1279–AD 1368)**—Mongol leader Genghis Khan conquered northern China in 1215, dividing the spoils among his four sons to rule. His grandson, Kublai Khan, defeated the Songs in 1279 and combined China with his grandfather's empire to form the Yuan dynasty, which spread from East China Sea across Asia to what is today Poland and Hungary.
- **Ming Dynasty (1368–AD 1644)**—General Zhu Yuanzhang forced the Mongols out of China. His son, Emperor Yongle, defeated the northern tribes and moved the capital of China to Beijing in 1403, where it has been ever since. He built the Imperial Palace, now known as the Forbidden City. Peasant uprisings, Japanese piracy, and Mongol tribe rebellions led to the downfall of the Ming dynasty.

- **Qing Dynasty (1644– AD 1911)**—Manchu tribes of the north captured Beijing in 1644, and China was once again ruled by a foreign-speaking people. The last of the Qing dynasty was infested with weak emperors and overbearing eunuchs. Plagued by its own internal Taiping Rebellion and two Opium Wars with Britain and its European allies, which resulted in Hong Kong ceded to Britain, the era of Chinese dynasties ended.

Being in 1898, a reform movement swept through China adapting Western election practices, technology, and education values that gradually undermined and caused the collapse of the Qing dynasty in 1911.

In the early twentieth centuries, the country was beset by civil unrest, major famines, military defeats, and foreign occupation. In 1931, Japan ruthlessly invaded Manchuria and by 1937 occupied much of northern China, Shanghai, and the Yangzi valley, causing massive death and destruction. Japan occupied China until kicked out by the allies during World War II. After World War II, the Communists under Mao Zedong established an autocratic socialist system that, while ensuring China's sovereignty, imposed strict controls over everyday life and cost the lives of tens of millions of people in what is now known as the Cultural Revolution. After 1978, his successor DENG Xiaoping and other leaders focused on stock market-oriented economic development, and by 2000 output had quadrupled. Today, political control remains tight; and there is no sign of the Communist Party relinquishing control, the room for personal choice has expanded, and the country has entered a period of economic prosperity. In fact, China is undergoing an amazing commercial and economic upheaval with Hong Kong–style cities popping up throughout the country—a new city every month.

Kenneth's Picks—Seldom Seen Exciting Places to Visit in China

Jade Dragon Snow Mountain seen from Black Dragon Pool.

1. **Shangri-La National Park**— In 1933, a British plane crashed somewhere in the Himalayas. The survivors had no idea where they were. They did know that it was a place of extraordinary beauty—a pure place of peace and tranquility. The survivors spoke of strange, wonderful experiences and mystic, illusionary, romantic experiences of having dreams come true. James Hilton authored the *Lost Horizon*, a successful novel turned into a Hollywood movie in 1937, about this place. Much of this mystic place is now a national park in China—Shangri-La National Park. It is an exciting place to visit. The Chinese government provides bus service to many of the remote lakes in the park, where interesting hiking trails circle each lake and tour boats take less ambitious visitors across the lakes.

2. **Jade Dragon Snow Mountain National Park**—Jade Dragon Snow Mountain is thirty-five kilometers (twenty-one miles) in length, consists of thirteen peaks over five thousand meters (16,400 feet) high, snow clad all year long, and surrounded by virgin pine and spruce forest. The thirteen peaks stand, one after the other, in a curved line that resembles the spiked back of a legendary Chinese fire-breathing dragon. Hence, the exotic name. The Chinese National Park Service has done an incredible job of building a cable car system to take visitors from the valley floor to the top of the Shangzhilu Mountain (5,595 meters)—the main attraction. The cable car drops visitors on top of a glacier, just below the peak at about five thousand one hundred meters. Bottles of oxygen can be purchased as you exit the cable car. From there a zigzag boardwalk, no doubt designed by the same architect that built the meandering Great Wall of China, leads the physically fit visitor to just below the top of the mountain at an elevation of 5,450 meters (17,876 feet). The views are sensational, and the experience unforgettable. But perhaps the best part of a visit to the park is the thrill of attending *Impression LiJiang*—an outstanding outdoor theater musical production, with a cast of a thousand well choreographed, that competes with the finest Broadway musicals. The park is located near LiJiang, Yunnan Province.

3. **Stone Forest National Park**—Is one of China's most unusual and newest national parks. Wavy-shaped, thin-edged limestone pillars, some thirty meters (one hundred feet) high, form tightly packed tall stone configurations that take bizarre shapes. They have equally bizarre names such as Wife Waiting Impatiently for Husband, Everlasting Fungus and Rhinoceros Gazing at the Moon. An added attraction of the park is its location surrounded by the colorful Sami tribe, who provide tour guide service in the park.

4. **Tiger Leaping Gorge National Park**—It is one of the top three deepest, narrowest, most breathtaking, and grandiose canyons in the world. The other two being the Grand Canyon in Arizona, USA, and the Yualou Sang, Tibet. Legend has it that a giant mythical tiger leaped from one shore of the gorge to the sleeping boulder in the center of the river and then

to the far bank. Buses from Shangri-La will take you to the gorge. It takes about a full day to climb down the three hundred meters (one thousand feet) and back up, and travel round-trip from Shangri-La.

5. **Li River Scenic National Monument**—If you enjoy viewing misty morning fog, amid bizarre limestone peaks, while slowly floating in luxury aboard a riverboat, then Li River Scenic National Monument is the place for you. The scenic section of the LiJiang River begins just north of Guilin. It flows 437 kilometers (262 miles) down to Yangshou. Spectacular riverboat tours can easily be arranged at your hotel in Guilin. An affordable and great place to stay in Guilin that is in *The Guinness Book of Records* for the tallest man-made waterfall is the Waterfall Hotel. Every evening a wall of water spills from the roof over a wall of the hotel to the sound of eerie classical Chinese music and a colorful light display. You will be picked up at your hotel early in the morning and driven by van to the riverboat loading dock. From there you will float in peace and tranquility for about six hours, past thousands of limestone pinnacles and beautiful traditional Chinese landscape, the kind you find painted on ancient Chinese scrolls. You will have about two hours to stroll about in the tourist town of Yangshou among the shops, boutiques, fast-food establishments, pubs and cafes, before boarding a bus to be driven back to your hotel. The bus ride back to Guilin takes about an hour and a half hours.

6. **LiJiang Old Town**—This is perhaps the quaintest, most peaceful, and charming village the author has ever had the good fortune to visit. LiJiang is a UN World Cultural Heritage Site. It was once an important town on the ancient Silk Road. It is nestled in a warm valley beneath the majestic mountains of Jade Dragon Snow Mountain National Park. Three parallel rivers, each originating at Snow Mountain pass by the Old Town. Several streams enter the Old Town, and water runs along the center of each street and lane; water is diverted into each resident's garden and under their villa to perfect feng shui, peace, health, and harmony. Hundreds of simple but elegant and enchanting foot bridges make passage from one side of the lane to the other a delight. Because the area is relatively warm in the winter, beautiful-patterned and colorful coy (*carp* to some, *coy* to others) survive all year long in the Old Town streams that pass through the streets.

7. **Beijing Attractions**—For a listing and description of recommended places to visit in and around Beijing see chapter 4.

CHINA
Guilin, Kunming, Nunning, LiJiang, Shangri-La, Tibet, Hong Kong, Macau

1. Guilin (pronounced Qee-Lynn) offers many beautiful examples of traditional Chinese architecture. Seen is Sun Pagoda made of copper.

2. Ooops . . . there's another one behind it. It is Moon Pagoda made of colorful blue tiles.

3. Double Bridge at Guilin's four lakes, that's Li (Lee) River Scenic National Park in the background.

4. Uniquely Chinese architectural elements, such multistory tapered roofs and curly cue corners, are well illustrated on this lakeside pagoda. Once used only as Buddhist temples, today pagodas appear without temples to bring good luck or prevent floods.

5 & 6. Day or night, night or day can't decide which looks best.

7. Don't miss the night cruise through the four lakes at Guilin. Do you like a gold or blue pagoda? Some prefer purple or pink.

8 & 9. A third pagoda-style Buddhist temple.

10. The purple pagoda is Disney in presentation, illumination, perfection, and with soft Oriental music background. It is crowned with a lotus blossom.

I've been asked, "Kenneth, what did you do in China?" See for yourself . . .

11. Visited a few fine friends.

12. Attended a few GREAT shows including DREAMLAND, which were as good as any in Las Vegas, New York, San Francisco, Paris, or London. Chinese-style musical acrobatics are second to none.

191

13 & 14. Enjoyed a home-cooked meal. If you enjoy Chinese takeout in the States, Europe, or elsewhere, you are going to flip over Chinese food served up in China.

15 & 16. Stayed out of trouble. Why the police march tandem, in groups of three, through the streets is one of life's mysteries. The white gloves are a nice touch. China has its share of human rights issues; but it's not noticeable on the content, happy, smiling faces we saw all over China. How's your tan? Mine's darker than yours!

17 & 18. Rented a car which got great mileage. That's the tiny red gas tank sitting on top of the engine block. Takes a really hard bounce to knock it off. Funny place for the license plate.

19 & 20. Helped out a local farmer, who looked down on his luck.

21 & 22. Went fishing, but caught no fish. Koi is a scarred fish cherished throughout Asia. Asians enjoy a moment of respite from today's fast-pace and sometimes stressful life by feeding koi at local lakes or ponds. *Kohaku* (Japanese name), the reddish orange and white koi are the most popular and especially loved by the Japanese whose national flag was designed based on *kohaku*'s colors.

23 & 24. Listened to street musicians and saw a new bird in the wild—the mandarin drake.

25 & 26. Stayed in five-star hotels for about $100 per night with breakfast. Chinese sign reads Entrance to Flower Gardens.

27 & 28. Hiked the soggy trails of Stone Forest National Park. Those aren't trees in the background; they are limestone pillars some one hundred feet high.

29 & 30. Attended a SPECTACULAR outdoor performance titled *LiJiang Impressions* with a cast of one thousand, all in traditional Chinese dress. The amphitheater is located at the entrance to Jade Dragon Snow Mountain National Park.

31 & 32. A cast of a thousand from fifty-seven tribes performed wearing brightly colored traditional native dress and sang cultural Oriental songs.

33 & 34. Witnessed some strange agricultural practices. Yes, that's corn hanging from the roof.

35 & 36. Went shopping. Ugh! But loved the traditional architecture—tile roofs with corners slanted up.

37 & 38. Enjoyed a quiet diner at LiJiang Old Town, place of famous three parallel rivers.

39 & 40. Couldn't interest these old Naxi tribe gals into some friendly chitchat. It's amazing how many people can speak English in China.

205

41 & 42. Made some new friends of all ages in Shangri-La.

43 & 44. Saw a variety of fine art—some I understood, some I didn't.

207

45 & 46. Cruised the Li River National Park and took great pleasure in the beautiful scenery, but choked on China's air pollution.

47 a, b, c. All-day cruises from Guilin to Yangshou takes eight hours and includes two hours free time to shop in touristy Yangshou. You're bused back. Another outstanding adventure.

209

49 & 50. We watched commercial fisherman with trained cormorant fish from dusk till dawn. With a rubber band tied around its neck, a cormorant dives, catches a fish too big to swallow, surfaces, and dumps it in his master's basket. The fisherman rewards the cormorant with a tiny fish it can swallow. How they stay balanced on that narrow stick of a boat is incredible.

51 a, b, and c. At Shangri-La National Park (twelve thousand feet). We were surprised to see so many flowers blooming in October.

52 & 53. We were also surprised to see Spanish moss at twelve thousand feet!

54 & 55. Climbed to the top of Jade Dragon Snow Mountain National Park 4,580 meters (15,350 feet) without supplemental oxygen. Perhaps the stair platform contractor used the same designer as the Great Wall of China team did five centuries ago.

56 & 57. Had a little help climbing the first few thousand meters. A wonderfully designed cable car carries visitors to four thousand three hundred meters (14,100 feet). Notice the rugged glacier.

58 & 59. What we first thought was the young farmer's brothers turned out to be his older sisters; hardworking people are the Chinese.

60 & 61. The bicycle is NOT dead in China, and you can get some great buys on used bikes.

62. Made another friend—an elegant Naxi tribe lady.

63 & 64. Witnessed some weird and wonderful, out-of-the-ordinary Tibetan crop harvest practice; that's wheat and barley hanging on those timber racks.

65. Potala Palace Lhasa, Tibet.

66 & 67. Enjoyed a pre-Chinese crackdown on Tibet and made a few special Tibetan friends.
We hope they're safe.

68 & 69. Another glimpse of Tibetan life; don't know what the men on the roof are up to. It is a neat rural farming community.

70 & 71. Had some fun, but pee-peed my pants on the roller coaster at Hong Kong Disneyland's Space Mountain.

72 & 73. Headwaters of the Yangtze River—Shangri La.

74 & 75. Practically fell to the bottom of Tiger Leaping Gore National Park and strenuously climbed back up in a single day.

76 & 77. Tiger LeapingGorge is the world's third largest behind the Grand Canyon, USA, and Yualou Sang, Tibet.

78 & 79. Some lazy people pay to be carried back up. Old-timer entrepreneur (below) is selling baked yams on the trail.

225

80 & 81. We toured China with a prestigious politician, who invited us to his home (below).

82. Our fisherman buddy is returning from a long night on the Li River. He's carrying his two fishing buddies—diving cormorants.

83. A lovely Stone Forest National Park Ranger wearing traditional Sani tribal dress.

84. Talented and lovely Tibetan innkeeper at Bed & Breakfast Inn with an open-air courtyard, where all meals are served in all sorts of weather. Small charcoal chair warmers are placed under your seat in cold weather.

85 & 86. We traveled by rail, land, and sea. Above, a hovercraft leaves Macau for Hong Kong every fifteen minutes, 24/7, in both directions, and carries two hundred passengers in comfort. One-way trip takes one hour.

87 & 88. Miles long, this fascinating modern cable-stay bridge connects Macau to Tapai island, where most of the new casinos are under construction.

89 & 90. We lost some money at the Palace, but won a bundle at the Sands.

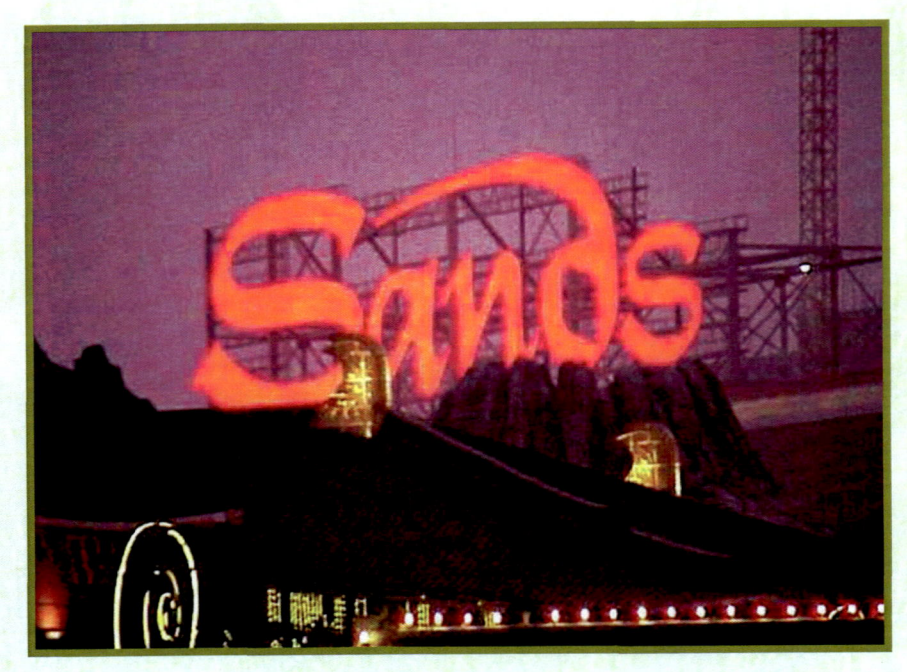

91 & 92. Casino craze has taken over Macau and Tapai island, China.

233

93. That's all, folks! Have fun! Soft landings from China.

Snapshot of the
2008 Beijing Summer Olympics

Cha-Mega-Adventure: Beijing 2008 Summer Olympic Games

Venues

China has been extremely generous and responsive to the needs of the games. China may have spent more money cuddling, embracing, competing, planning, organizing, designing, building, training, securing, operating, maintaining, entertaining, and financing the 2008 Beijing Summer Olympic Games than any other Olympics organization in history. China possibly spent more money than the USA and its coalition forces spent reconstructing Afghanistan and Iraq in 2007, which topped ten billion US dollars. As it stands today, it appears China spent its money well for an international worldwide cause that benefits all people throughout the world. China designed and built approximately thirty new stadiums and sports complex venues, as well as athlete housing and other related security and infrastructure projects that are dedicated exclusively to the success of the 2008 Olympic Games.

China offered, and the Olympic committee, somewhat overwhelmed by China's financial commitment, graciously accepted games played in a host of distinct venues including Beijing, Hong Kong, Shanghai, Tianjin, Shenyang, Qingdao, Lao Shan, and Qinhuangdao. A massive effort of planning, engineering, demolition, design, and construction took place to build thirty entirely new modern stadiums and all the related security, transportation, accommodations, and infrastructure necessary for a successful *cha-mega-adventure*. Massive new transportation, projects, housing, and security for the athletes, families, dignitaries, sponsors, spectators, and tourists alike were all accomplished in record-setting time. New billion-dollar stadiums popped up all over China—they are fairy dreams come true! All are fine examples of modern Oriental architecture; they are practical and simple but elegant. They flow with grace and class.

China can rightfully feel proud and deserves world recognition for an Olympic preparation job well done!

Some of the most prominent new venues are the following:

Shenyang Olympic Sports Ctr. Stadium

Qingdao International Marina

Hong Kong Equestrian Stadium

Tianjin Olympic Center Stadium

Shanghai Stadium
CTF

Beijing Shooting Range
Shooting

Beijing Inst of Technology Gym
Volleyball

Beijing University Gymnasium

Fencing Hall
Fencing

Yingdong Natatorium
Water Polo

Lao Shan Mountain Bike Course
Biking

Olympic Sports Center Gymnasium
Handball

Workers Indoor Arena

Capital Indoor Stadium
Volleyball

Fengtai Softball Field
Softball

Beijing Worker's Stadium
Football

Beijing Olympic Green Tennis Courts
Tennis

Beijing University of Technology Gym
Badminton, Gymnastics

Olympic Sports Center Stadium
Pentathlon – running and equestrian

China Agricultural Univ. Gymnasium
Wrestling

Peking University Gymnasium
Table Tennis

Beijing Science and Technology Univ. Gymnasium
Judo, Taekwondo

Wukesong Indoor Stadium

Lao Shan Velodrome
Cycling

Shunyi Olympic Rowing-Canoeing Park
Canoe, Kayak, Slalom

National Indoor Stadium
Gymnastics

Beijing Shooting Range Hall
Shooting

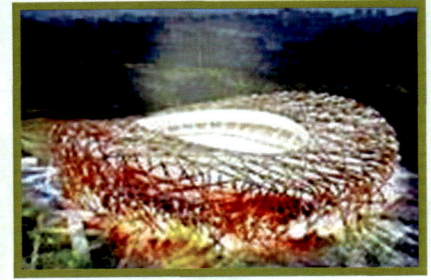

National Stadium
Opening Ceremony, Football, Athletics

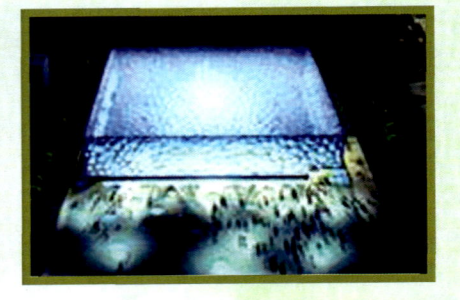

National Aquatics Center
Swimming, Diving

Qinhuangdao Olympic Sports Center

Where to Go in and Around Beijing and Other Interesting Sites

The Forbidden City

Hall of Supreme Harmony

The Forbidden City lies at the center of Beijing; called Gu Gong in Chinese, it was the Imperial Palace during the Ming and Qing dynasties. It is the biggest and best preserved complex of ancient buildings in China, and with 9,999 rooms, it is the largest palace complex in the world. It is a great place to start a tour of Beijing because Beijing was designed in concentric circles around the Forbidden City. The Forbidden City was in fine feng shui as it was considered the center of the universe and thus in perfect harmony with nature and the cosmos. Chinese geomancy, or feng shui, is based on ideas that the appropriate layout of a building or room affects the flow of qi, the cosmic breath of life and, hence, the inhabitants' well-being. From the Forbidden City it is an easy walk to the following: Tian'anmen Square, the Temple of Heaven, the Memorial Hall of Chairman Mao and Qian Men Gate, and a short cab ride to the Summer Palace, which are all described below.

The Gate of Heavenly Peace is the main entrance to the Forbidden City. Appearing on banknotes and stamps its icon is a famous Chinese icon recognized around the world. Hanging from the gate and facing Tian'anmen Square is a portrait of Mao; it is from a high platform on this gate that Mao delivered his liberation speech on October 1, 1949.

Entrance was a privilege allowed for only the closest relatives of the emperor and people working there. Ordinary people were forbidden from even approaching the walls of the palace; hence, it got the nickname the Forbidden City. Twenty-four Ming and Qing emperors reigned from here for nearly five hundred years. From 1420 to 1920, emperors ruled China with absolute authority. The emperor lived here with his family and as many as two thousand concubines, and an assortment of eunuchs and servants. As a preventive measure to ensure the authenticity of the emperor's children, eunuchs were the only male servants allowed in the Forbidden City. Confucius taught that self-disfigurement of the body would prevent access into the afterlife. Hence, in the hope of being buried whole when they died, eunuchs carried their testicles in leather bags hung from their belt.

Guided tours are given everyday.

Tain'amien Square

Covering more than forty hectares, Tain'anmen Square is the largest, perhaps most well-known, public gathering place among the world's prominent cities. A plain, flat, spacious, concrete slab, T-Square is surrounded by some of China's most-valued treasures and well-visited tourist attractions: the Forbidden City on the north side, Great Hall of the People to the west, Museum of Chinese History and Museum of the Revolution on the east, and ancient Qianmen Gate to the south. The massive plain and basic square has a military atmosphere with no softball, kite flying, or Frisbee tossing that leaves some people cold but others with a strong impression of China's history, culture, and contemporary political power. In 1976, at the center of T-Square, over a million volunteers helped erect Chairmen Mao Memorial Hall, which is open daily to the public. Historically, T-Square has been a place of pilgrimage, where millions have met to discuss social issues. Some well-known historic meetings at the Square are the following:

- May 4, 1919—The first recorded public meeting took place when thousands of students converged on T-Square to protest the terms of the Versailles Treaty that ended World War I. After the Chinese sacrificed, suffering great hardship, and over one hundred thousand Chinese volunteered to help the French and British maintain supply lines, the treaty awarded Chinese lands to the Japanese. China was outraged.
- 1925—Thousands protested the massacre of Chinese demonstrators in Shanghai by British troops.
- 1926—Thousands met at T-Square, this time to challenge the Chinese government's weak handling of affairs with occupying Japanese forces. This was the first time demonstrators were fired on by the Chinese military.
- 1976—The death of popular premier Zhou Enlai prompted a massive rally of mourners to assemble, without government permission, to protest their dissatisfaction with the new leaders of government.
- 1978—Groups met to discuss new ideas of freedom, democracy, artistic freewill, independence, and inventiveness.
- 1987—Students and other supporters gathered to protest the government's refusal to allow elections.
- 1989—The Grand Finale of massive public dissent took place on T-Square when millions of students and others met to discuss, demonstrate, and protest the absence of reform, censorship, government corruption, and lack of freedom. Refusing the government's order to disband or to observe the declaration of martial law, protesters camped out on T-Square in tents, from April until that dreadful night on June 4 when the tanks rolled in. In the closing moments that night, tanks ran over tents, machine guns fired randomly into the screaming crowd, and troops chased fleeing civilians and shot them dead. No one knows how many thousands of lives were lost; the government isn't saying how many were killed or imprisoned.

The Great Wall of China

One of the most visited places in China, the Great Wall (221–210 BC) is about four thousand miles (6,350 kilometers) long; it snakes its way across the mountains and valleys of five provinces in Northern China. It was built in stages as a mammoth defense barricade during the Qin dynasty. Unfortunately, most of the wall has disintegrated by the forces of nature or at the hand of man. A study done in 2002 by the China Great Wall Academy concluded that only 30 percent of the wall remains intact. The best preserved, most imposing section, and choice place to view the wall is at Badaling, Beijing, which is about forty-five miles (seventy-five kilometers) from Beijing's city center. There you will find a visitor center and great movie about the construction and history of the wall. This restored section can be walked for about half mile (one kilometer) long before it disintegrates into rumble.

The Great Wall has long been incorporated into Chinese mythology and popular symbolism. The most beautiful of several legends is about the collapse of a section of the Great Wall caused by Meng Jiang Nu, who cried bitterly over the death of her husband during the construction of the Great Wall. This legend has spread widely through China via textbooks, folk songs, and traditional operas.

Temple of Heaven

The Temple of Heaven in the southern part of Beijing is China's largest existing complex of ancient sacrificial buildings. Occupying an area of 273 hectares, it is three times the area of the Forbidden City. It was built in 1420 for emperors to worship heaven. The principal buildings include the Altar of Prayer for Good Harvests, Imperial Vault of Heaven, and Circular Mound Altar.

The Altar of Prayer for Good Harvest, thirty-eight meters in height and thirty meters in diameter, stands on a round foundation built with three levels of marble stones. This towering triple-eave hall is under a three-story, cone-shaped glaze-tile roof in blue color crowned with a gilded knob. A circular wall of polished bricks known as the Echo Wall encloses the Imperial Vault of Heaven. The Circular Mount Altar, south to the Imperial Vault of Heaven, is where the emperor prayed to heaven. At the center lies a round stone called the Center of Heaven Stone that echoes when a visitor speaks loudly when standing on the stone.

The Temple of Heaven is located one-fourth mile (two kilometers) from Tiananmen Square.

The Memorial Hall of Chairman Mao

The Memorial Hall of Chairman Mao is located in the geographic center of Tian'anmen Square and is the home of the pickled corpse of Chairman Mao. The public is allowed to queue and walk past Mao's crystal coffin. Mechanically raised from a freezer each morning, Mao's corpse is draped with a Chinese red flag and looks unreal like it was made of caulk or wax. The atmosphere is reverent, there is no talking, and no cameras are allowed inside the hall. Show disrespect and you'll be at the airport and out of China in a heartbeat.

The Summer Palace

Old Summer Palace in Traditional Chinese Painting

The **Old Summer Palace** originally called the **Imperial Gardens**, known in China as the **Gardens of Perfect Clarity** (a popular name in China was the Garden of Gardens), was a complex of palaces and but best known for its extensive collection of gardens and building architectures and other works of art. Located five miles (eight kilometers) northwest of Beijing's city center, it was built in the eighteenth and early nineteenth century, where the emperors of the Qing dynasty resided and handled government affairs. Beijing is a griddle in the summer, an icebox in the winter. Emperors would depart the Forbidden City in the spring to avoid the hot Beijing summers and spend it at the cooler Kunming Lake. The central Kunming Lake, covering 2.2 square kilometers, was entirely man-made, and the excavated soil was used to build Longevity Hill.

The Imperial Gardens were entirely destroyed by troops from Britain and France. Today, the destruction of the Gardens of Perfect Brightness is still regarded as a symbol of foreign aggression and humiliation in China.

In 1860, during the Second Opium War, British and French expeditionary forces, having marched inland from the coast, reached Beijing (then known as Peking). On the night of October 6–7, French units diverted from the main attack force towards to the Old Summer Palace. Although the French commander, Montauban, assured the British commander, Grant, that "nothing had been touched," extensive looting, also undertaken by British and Chinese, took place. The Old Summer Palace was only now occupied by a few eunuchs, the emperor Xianfeng having run away. There was no significant resistance to the looting from the Chinese, even though many Chinese Imperial soldiers were in the surrounding country. On October 18, 1860, the British high commissioner to China, Lord Elgin, decided to destroy the Old Summer Palace as a means to punish the emperor Xianfeng without harming the general population, or destroying Beijing itself, for the sanctioned torture and murder of almost twenty Western prisoners, including two British envoys and a journalist for the *Times*.

Charles George Gordon, a twenty-seven-year-old captain in the Royal Engineers Corps wrote the following:

> We went out, and, after pillaging it, burned the whole place, destroying in a vandal-like manner most valuable property which [could] not be replaced for millions . . . The [local] people are very civil, but I think they hate us, as they must after what we did to the Palace. You can scarcely imagine the beauty and magnificence of the places we burnt. It made one's heart sore to burn them; in fact, these places were so large, and we were so pressed for time, that we could not plunder then carefully. Quantities of gold ornaments were burnt, considered as brass. It was wretchedly demoralizing work for an army.

Today, much of the Old Summer Palace and Gardens have been restored to their former elegance and beauty and well worth a visit.

Qian Men Gate

Qian Men or Front Gate is a striking fifteenth-century double-arched gate of extraordinary pagoda-style Oriental architecture at the south end of Tian'anmen Square. The larger of the two gate towers, locally known as Zhengyang Men, is 131 feet (forty meters) high and now home to Beijing History Museum. Its sister Jian Lou or Arrow Tower is 125 feet (thirty-eight meters). During the Qing dynasty, there were nine such gates controlling passage from the Chinese residential quarters and the Forbidden City. Today, Qian Men is the last remaining gate and symbolic entry to Beijing's newest entertainment quarter filled with silk traders, bakeries, street stalls, herbal shops, cinemas, clubs, restaurants, and sidewalk artists.

The southernmost Arrow Tower (Jian Lou) is no longer open to the public. You can, however, still climb up inside the rear building, called the Zhengyang Men, where an enjoyable photo exhibition depicts life in Beijing's pre-1949 markets, temples, and *hutong*.

Terracotta Army

Near the ancient historic capital of China, Xi'an, the celebrated Terracotta Army still stands guard over the tomb of Emperor Qin Shi Huang. In 1974, workers digging a well discovered the underground army. The full-size Terracotta Army consists of horse soldiers, infantry, archers, and four-horse chariots are all in surprisingly great condition. It is reported that Emperor Qin Shi Huang spared no expense and enlisted over seven thousand craftsmen that spent thirty-four years building the army.

Acknowledgments and Picture Credit

During my years of research, writing, traveling, and photographing, in preparation for producing this book, I have been fortunate in the assistance I have received from family, friends, and fellow colleagues and would like to express to them my deepest gratitude. I am especially indebted to Chun Ming Foo, owner of Creative Edge, an outstanding graphic artist, computer metrics expert, and wonderful giving man for many favors, large and small, and his research and support in obtaining information about Malaysian natural history and culture.

I am grateful for the contribution other professional photographers have made and herein acknowledge their individual photo credits:

Accomplished German photographer Alfred Molon (www:Molon.de) for his photos of Bako National Park, Malaysia; Li River, Guilin, China; and orangutans, Sabah, Malaysia;

Zhang Liping, Guilin landscape photographer (glzlp616@263.net) for a few fisherman photos taken along the Lijiang River, China.

Loon Woon, Borneo naturalist photographer for a few photos of Sarawak, Malaysia.

Webmaster@China.Org.CN—Panda Photo. (Every effort was made to contact the copyright holders. My e-mails and letter seeking permission to use this fine panda photo went unanswered. Hence, I herein offer a special thanks and appreciation to the unknown photographer.)

Sarawak Tourist Board for their permission to use some of their fine photos of Sarawak.

Facts, statistics, population, and geographic data such as the number of islands in the Philippines and percentage of islands uninhabited were obtained from the Web site: http//www.CIA.Worldfactbook.com. It is a superb site with information about all 194 countries on the planet. And it is a public domain, so go there and help yourself. Another excellent Web site with free public domain information and photos that the author found excellent and would like to thank is WWW.en.Wikipedia.org: *The Free Encyclopedia*, folks.

I am especially thankful to the Malaysian, Chinese, and Philippine governments for allowing me free access to travel throughout their countries, explore their natural wonders, speak with the local people, and photograph their many wonderful landscapes and treasures.

I would also like to thank the China Internet Information Center for its wealth of public domain information pertaining to all manner of subjects from Chinese history, economics, and culture; to travel modes; and interesting places to visit and accommodations.

All of the beautiful orchards photographed herein were grown by the author's good friend Loon Woon and his lovely wife at their home in Kuching.

About the Author

Field of Lupines, Iceland, June 2006

Mr. Brophy is a civil structural engineer, float pilot, and "birder." He is the author of *America's National Parks: How Well Do You Know Them?*, a new novel *Anneee*, and coauthor of *Stories of the Unexpected*, which won Florida Best Book Award 2003. He has visited 366 of America's 389 national park sites, enjoyed each and every visit, and discovered something unique and interesting at each site. Besides visiting all fifty states, he has traveled to 116 countries and made sure to visit at least one national park in each. He is working on his next book, "The World's Greatest Parks." He has a summer home in South Paris, Maine, a winter home in Port Charlotte, Florida, and spends considerable time with the Foo clan in Kuching, Malaysia. He spent 2004, 2005, and 2006 in Iraq designing and building schools, power plants, primary healthcare clinics, and hospitals. He is currently in Afghanistan consulting for the U.S. Department of State, International Narcotics and Law Enforcement Affairs building regional training centers for police mentoring.